I0015475

Swift 2 Blueprints

Sharpen your skills in Swift by designing and deploying seven fully-functional applications

Cecil Costa

BIRMINGHAM - MUMBAI

Swift 2 Blueprints

Copyright © 2015 Packt Publishing

All rights reserved. No part of this book may be reproduced, stored in a retrieval system, or transmitted in any form or by any means, without the prior written permission of the publisher, except in the case of brief quotations embedded in critical articles or reviews.

Every effort has been made in the preparation of this book to ensure the accuracy of the information presented. However, the information contained in this book is sold without warranty, either express or implied. Neither the author, nor Packt Publishing, and its dealers and distributors will be held liable for any damages caused or alleged to be caused directly or indirectly by this book.

Packt Publishing has endeavored to provide trademark information about all of the companies and products mentioned in this book by the appropriate use of capitals. However, Packt Publishing cannot guarantee the accuracy of this information.

First published: October 2015

Production reference: 1211015

Published by Packt Publishing Ltd.
Livery Place
35 Livery Street
Birmingham B3 2PB, UK.

ISBN 978-1-78398-076-5

www.packtpub.com

Credits

Author
Cecil Costa

Reviewers
Eugene Mozharovsky

Alexey Smirnov

Jak Tiano

Commissioning Editor
Dipika Gaonkar

Acquisition Editors
Larissa Pinto

Sam Wood

Content Development Editor
Zeeyan Pinheiro

Technical Editor
Shivani Kiran Mistry

Copy Editor
Akshata Lobo

Project Coordinator
Suzanne Coutinho

Proofreader
Safis Editing

Indexer
Monica Ajmera Mehta

Graphics
Disha Haria

Production Coordinator
Arvindkumar Gupta

Cover Work
Arvindkumar Gupta

About the Author

Cecil Costa, also known as Eduardo Campos in Latin countries, is a Euro-Brazilian freelance developer who has been learning about computers since he got his first PC (an AT 286) in 1990. From then on, he kept learning about programming languages, computer architecture, and computer science theory.

Learning and teaching are his passions; this is the reason why he worked as a trainer and an author. He has been giving on-site courses for companies such as Ericsson, Roche, TVE (a Spanish television channel), and a lot of other companies. He is also the author of *Swift Cookbook* and soon he will also write a book called *Reactive Swift Programming*.

Nowadays, he teaches through online platforms, helping people from every part of the world.

In 2008, he founded his own company, Conglomo Limited (`http://www.conglomo.es/`), which offers development and training programs both on site and online.

Over his professional career, he has created projects by himself and also worked for different companies, from small to big ones, such as IBM, Qualcomm, Spanish Lottery, and DIA%.

He develops a variety of computer languages (such as Swift, C++, Java, Objective-C, JavaScript, Python, and so on) in different environments (iOS, Android, Web, Mac OS X, Linux, Unity, and so on) because he thinks that a good developer needs to learn every kind of programming language to open his mind, and only then will he really know what development is.

Nowadays, Cecil is based in the UK, where he is progressing in his professional career, working with augmented reality on mobile platforms.

I would like to thank Mr Robert William Bemer for creating the escape key and my son Gabriel Campos Oliveira for bringing happiness to my life.

About the Reviewers

Eugene Mozharovsky started his computer science journey in 2010 with a school course on programming in Pascal. Then, he explored Java for himself and it was the whole world of object-oriented programming, a full-featured API, and powerful client-server techniques. In 2013, he switched to Mac OS and found his true passion in app development for Apple mobile devices. In summer 2014, he fell in love with Swift and iOS 8 beta and is currently working on a handy social app. When he doesn't code, he tries to systematize physics for his own understanding of how the Universe works or train his exotic parrots.

Alexey Smirnov works as a software engineer at a small start up company called iRONYUN (`http://ironyun.com`). In his spare time, he enjoys building iOS apps using Objective-C and Swift. Alexey got his master's degree in computer science from Stony Brook University, USA.

Jak Tiano is a mobile designer and programmer. He specializes in mobile game development using Unity3D, but also works with countless other engines. He has been developing iOS applications since 2008, and has been all-in on Swift since its release in 2014. He works as a freelance mobile developer, and co-runs not a hipster coffee shop, an independent game studio in Burlington, VT.

> I'd like to thank the great people at Packt for giving me the opportunity to contribute to this book and Taylor Swift for frequently providing the background music for my review sessions.

www.PacktPub.com

Support files, eBooks, discount offers, and more

For support files and downloads related to your book, please visit www.PacktPub.com.

Did you know that Packt offers eBook versions of every book published, with PDF and ePub files available? You can upgrade to the eBook version at www.PacktPub.com and as a print book customer, you are entitled to a discount on the eBook copy. Get in touch with us at service@packtpub.com for more details.

At www.PacktPub.com, you can also read a collection of free technical articles, sign up for a range of free newsletters and receive exclusive discounts and offers on Packt books and eBooks.

https://www2.packtpub.com/books/subscription/packtlib

Do you need instant solutions to your IT questions? PacktLib is Packt's online digital book library. Here, you can search, access, and read Packt's entire library of books.

Why subscribe?

- Fully searchable across every book published by Packt
- Copy and paste, print, and bookmark content
- On demand and accessible via a web browser

Free access for Packt account holders

If you have an account with Packt at www.PacktPub.com, you can use this to access PacktLib today and view 9 entirely free books. Simply use your login credentials for immediate access.

Table of Contents

Preface

Swift, a relatively new computer language created by Apple Computers and its version 2 was already released. This programming language is gradually gaining features, performance, and stability. This book shows you how to create different apps using different frameworks. Thus, after reading this book, you will have a big skill set for Swift development.

What this book covers

Chapter 1, *Exploring Xcode*, explores some features of Xcode. It gives you some tips on how to debug and develop more quickly.

Chapter 2, *Creating a City Information App with Customized Table Views*, shows you how to create an app with different scenes and table views, retrieving information from the Internet. Here, you will learn how to use SwiftyJSON, a framework that allows you to work with JSON messages very easily.

Chapter 3, *Creating a Photo Sharing App*, will show you how to use the camera, edit your photo, and share it with your friends using the social framework.

Chapter 4, *Simulating Home Automation with HomeKit*, will show you how to simulate a house with its devices, create an app that retrieves your devices' information, and also change their state. This kind of app will be popular very soon due to the popularity of the Internet of Things (IoT).

Chapter 5, *Health Analyzing App Using HealthKit*, will teach you how to use HealthKit. Here, you are going to do some queries to receive and update the user's health data. You will appreciate a different way of treating the data as it needs to be converted into your favorite unit. Besides this, you will learn a third-party framework called iOS Chart. Here, you will be able to display some charts to the user to check their progress.

Chapter 6, Creating a Game App Using SpriteKit, is a chapter for those who like playing games on their phones. It is even more fun when you learn how to create your game, mainly if it is with SpriteKit, a framework that is very easy to follow and made for developing 2D games. We will develop a game based on a surfer dinosaur that needs to dodge the enemies. To move the character, we will use the accelerometer sensor.

Chapter 7, Creating an Apple Watch App, shows us how to create an app that controls our fridge. We can check our Apple Watch for the amount of food that we still have. This app also helps us display the route on the map to the supermarket.

Chapter 8, AVFoundation, shows how your phone, besides recording videos, can also edit them. Here, we are going to use a low-level framework called AVFoundation to change the audio of an existing video from the photos gallery. To do this app, we will also need some help from the photos framework.

What you need for this book

As you are developing iOS apps, you will need a relatively new Apple computer with OS X Yosemite (10.10) or above, Xcode 6 or above, and for some chapters, a physical Apple mobile device would be needed, because some features are not supported by the simulator. A few cases will require you to be enrolled in the Apple Developer Program due to the requirement of some capabilities. An Internet connection is also required for some chapters.

Who this book is for

You! That's right, if you are an iOS developer and you want to do some real-life examples using the Swift programming language. If you are willing to learn a big variety of iOS frameworks, this is the right book for you, as we are going to develop seven apps using different frameworks.

Conventions

In this book, you will find a number of text styles that distinguish between different kinds of information. Here are some examples of these styles and an explanation of their meaning.

Code words in text, database table names, folder names, filenames, file extensions, pathnames, dummy URLs, user input, and Twitter handles are shown as follows: " Now it time to develop the viewDidLoad method."

A block of code is set as follows:

```
class Person{
    var name:String
    var age:Int
    init(name: String, age:Int) {
        self.name = name
        self.age = age
    }
}
```

When we wish to draw your attention to a particular part of a code block, the relevant lines or items are set in bold:

```
class Person{
    var name:String
    var age:Int
    var address:String
    init(name: String, age:Int) {
        self.name = name
        self.age = age
    }
}
```

New terms and **important words** are shown in bold. Words that you see on the screen, for example, in menus or dialog boxes, appear in the text like this: "Clicking the **Next** button moves you to the next screen."

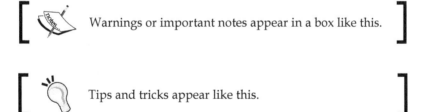

Warnings or important notes appear in a box like this.

Tips and tricks appear like this.

Reader feedback

Feedback from our readers is always welcome. Let us know what you think about this book — what you liked or disliked. Reader feedback is important for us as it helps us develop titles that you will really get the most out of.

To send us general feedback, simply e-mail feedback@packtpub.com, and mention the book's title in the subject of your message.

If there is a topic that you have expertise in and you are interested in either writing or contributing to a book, see our author guide at www.packtpub.com/authors.

Customer support

Now that you are the proud owner of a Packt book, we have a number of things to help you to get the most from your purchase.

Downloading the example code

You can download the example code files from your account at http://www.packtpub.com for all the Packt Publishing books you have purchased. If you purchased this book elsewhere, you can visit http://www.packtpub.com/support and register to have the files e-mailed directly to you.

Downloading the color images of this book

We also provide you with a PDF file that has color images of the screenshots/diagrams used in this book. The color images will help you better understand the changes in the output. You can download this file from https://www.packtpub.com/sites/default/files/downloads/Swift_2_Blueprints_ColorImages.pdf.

Errata

Although we have taken every care to ensure the accuracy of our content, mistakes do happen. If you find a mistake in one of our books—maybe a mistake in the text or the code—we would be grateful if you could report this to us. By doing so, you can save other readers from frustration and help us improve subsequent versions of this book. If you find any errata, please report them by visiting http://www.packtpub.com/submit-errata, selecting your book, clicking on the **Errata Submission Form** link, and entering the details of your errata. Once your errata are verified, your submission will be accepted and the errata will be uploaded to our website or added to any list of existing errata under the Errata section of that title.

To view the previously submitted errata, go to https://www.packtpub.com/books/content/support and enter the name of the book in the search field. The required information will appear under the **Errata** section.

Piracy

Piracy of copyrighted material on the Internet is an ongoing problem across all media. At Packt, we take the protection of our copyright and licenses very seriously. If you come across any illegal copies of our works in any form on the Internet, please provide us with the location address or website name immediately so that we can pursue a remedy.

Please contact us at `copyright@packtpub.com` with a link to the suspected pirated material.

We appreciate your help in protecting our authors and our ability to bring you valuable content.

Questions

If you have a problem with any aspect of this book, you can contact us at `questions@packtpub.com`, and we will do our best to address the problem.

1
Exploring Xcode

Programming is not only about code, it is also about methodology. It doesn't matter how many years you've been programming with Xcode, there is always a new feature that can speed up your development, mainly nowadays that there is a new version every few months. Don't forget that Swift is a new language created to replace the old Objective-C, which means that Xcode also needs to adopt new features for this new programming language.

This book is about creating applications with the Swift programming language using Xcode 6 as an IDE. The idea behind these apps is to show how to create different kinds of real apps from scratch and this chapter presents with you some tricks on how to use Xcode.

Even if you are already a developer with years of experience in Xcode, it is worth reading this chapter because there is always a different way to do a task and it can be very helpful. So, let's start reviewing some Xcode and Swift features. In this chapter, we will cover:

- Keyboard shortcuts
- Versioning your project
- Testing with Playground
- Debugging
- New Swift features
- Some final comments

Keyboard shortcuts

Have you ever thought of how much time a developer expends in moving the mouse pointer? It can be a lot of time. How about reducing some time by memorizing a few key combinations. Of course, don't expect to memorize all of them in a day. You can practice them when it is necessary; you will see that, after a while, you will save a lot of time. Of course, *command + X, command + C, command + V*, and *command + Q* are not going to be mentioned for they are assumed to be known.

The first shortcut we are going to learn is *command + B*, which is to build the solution without running it on the device or simulator. This key combination is very useful when you want to check whether the project has any errors, but you don't want to waste time installing the app.

Sometimes, mainly when you have Swift and C on the same project, the compiler caches the object files wrongly, so the best solution would be to clean everything up and recompile again. To clean your entire project, use the *command + shift + K* combination. Cleaning is a fast process, nevertheless, you have to remember that afterward you need to rebuild your project, which might take a while.

If you want to build your product and run it, you have two options. The first is *command + R* that compiles your project if it is necessary and installs it on the device or simulator; this combination is equivalent to pressing play on the left-hand side of the toolbar. The second option is *control + command + R*, which installs the last build but doesn't rebuild the project; it is very handy when your project takes a long time to compile and you just want to reinstall it again for testing.

Now, let's learn some key combinations that will affect Xcode, visually speaking. On the left-hand side, we have the Navigator. As you know, here is where you can access the project files, the search results, and the compilation status. The following screenshot shows a sample of the Navigator:

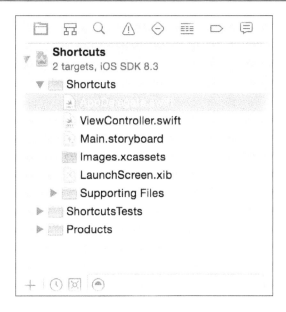

If you need more visual space, you can hide the Navigator area with *command + 0*, or you can show this area using the same combination. It is very useful when you have a small screen like a MacBook screen and you need to work with the interface builder or Playground.

As you can see, there is a bar on the top (called the Navigator bar), which allows you to access different sections of the Navigator. You can click on each icon or you can save some time by pressing *command +* a number from *1* to *8*, *1* being the project navigator (folder icon), *2* the symbol navigator, and so on till *8*, which is the report navigator.

Every Navigator section has a text field at the bottom to filter the content that is being displayed on the Navigator. You can reach this text field very fast by using the *command + option + J* combination. So, based on the previous combination, when you need to access a file, you can go to the project navigator by pressing *command + 1* followed by *command + option + J*.

To finish with the Navigator area, you should know that you have a shortcut to go to the project navigator and highlight the current file, it is *command + shift + J*.

The area on the right-hand side is called the Utility area and its combinations are similar to the Navigator area. This area can be hidden or shown with *command + option + 0*, its sections can be accessed with *command + option + a number from 1 to 6*, and its filter can be reached with *command + option + L*. The following screenshot is a sample of the Utility area:

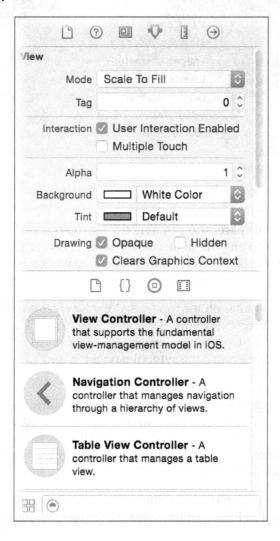

The area located between the Navigators and the Utility area at the bottom of the Xcode screen is called the Debug area. This area can be shown or hidden with *command* + *shift* + *Y*. Here, you have some debug combinations like *command* + *Y* to enable or disable breakpoints or pause or resume the application with *control* + *command* + *Y*. There are more debugging keyboard shortcuts; as they require the use of *fn* keys (*F6*, *F7*, *F8*), it can be complicated according to your keyboard. Here, you have a sample of the Debug area:

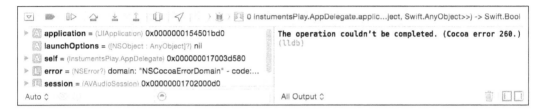

Now, the central area, which is the most important one, is called the Editor area. Here, as you know, is where you type your code. Scrolling up and down could waste a lot of time, so let's learn some shortcuts that will make us find our code faster. The first combination is *command* + *F* that opens a text field to search in the current file.

When you need to search in the whole project, you can use the *command* + *shift* + *F* combination, which is much faster than a click on the loupe icon and a click on the text field. Another similar combination is *command* + *shift* + *O* (letter *O*, not the number zero), which is called **Open Quickly...**. This combination opens a text field in front of your editor area and allows you to search for symbols. It also allows you to type the first letter of each symbol word, like the following example in which NSHD was typed and it was able to find **NSHomeDirectory**.

Open Quickly searches for symbols in the current project and also inside the frameworks. But if you like to jump to a symbol (method, property, global variable, and so on), you can use *control + 6* as it opens the combo box that is located at the top of the editor area like in the following screenshot:

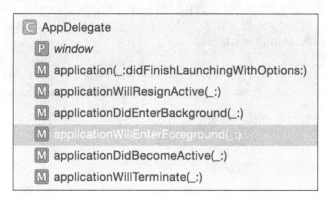

To navigate through the files you've been using, you can use *control + command + ←* to go to the previous files or *control + command + →* for the next one. Alternatively, you can slide with two fingers on use the touch pad if you have one.

When you have a code that is quite difficult to understand because it is not well-formatted, you can use the *control + I* combination. If you have selected some lines, only these lines will be arranged. If no line is selected, then the current line of code will be formatted.

To finish this shortcuts section, it is worth mentioning that you have *command + * to toggle breakpoints and *command + /* to toggle the selected line comments.

Don't worry if you think that there are too many combinations to memorize or if some of them are hard to do, you can always check the combination and customize it if you want by opening the Xcode menu, selecting preferences, and opening the **Key Bindings** section like in the following screenshot:

 Bear in mind while customizing your shortcuts that when you work on another computer, you will have to set them up again.

Versioning your project

Every project should have a version control system, even if you are the only developer. Xcode works with Git as a default VCS, which has a special way of working.

Firstly, you have to know that Xcode offers you just the basic usage of Git; there are times when you might need to use the command line.

You can use Git in two ways: locally only or remote and locally. The first one is usually done by single developers and can be done very easily by checking this option when you have to select a folder for your new project. The following screenshot shows the option that needs to be checked in the file dialog:

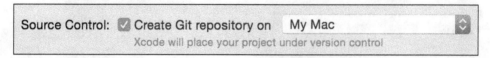

The second way of working with Git is to use it remotely and locally. What does it mean? It means that you can create versions of your code locally and when you think that it is ready to be shared with the other members of the team, you can send it to the server. To do so, you have to configure a server by yourself or you can use this service from a third-party company, such as GitHub or BitBucket.

 Recently, Apple announced the Xcode server, where you can configure your Git server and also a continuous integration system. Explaining how to configure this server can be very exhausting and is out of the scope of this book. However, if you would like to create your own server, you can have a look at this possibility.

As a developer what you need to work with a remote repository is its URL. You have to request it to the system administrator or you can copy it from the website where you created it. GitHub, for example, shows it on the right-hand side with a button to copy the URL on the clipboard, as you can see in the following screenshot:

Once you have the URL, you can check it out by selecting the **Check out an existing project** option on the start up screen, as shown in the following screenshot. Or, you can click on the **Source Control** menu and select the **Check out...** option.

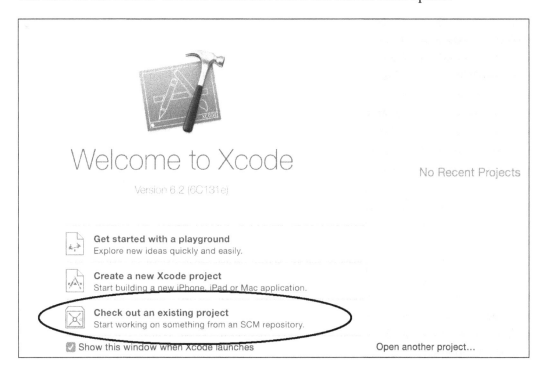

Once you have your project checked out and have started working on it, it doesn't matter whether it was created from a server or locally only. You will notice that when a file is modified, letter **M** will appear next to your file name on the project navigator. Letter **A** will also appear when a new file is added to the project. The next screenshot shows a sample of some files that were added or modified:

Note that letter **M** can also appear next to your project; it means that something in the project.pbxproj file, which is inside of your project package. This file contains the information of your project like the source code files with their path and the settings; hence, you have to deliver it every time you add a file or change any setting.

To commit the modified and new files, you just need to use the *command + option + C* key combination. A dialog asking for a description of the modifications will appear, leave a message in a way that another developer understands what was done.

> Avoid committing without leaving a comment, or just leaving a nonexpressive comment like "modifications." Comments are very useful to check the project's progress and fix bugs.

These commits are done locally by default. It means that only your computer knows about your modifications. If you want to send your commits to the server, don't forget to check the option that is under the comment box, as it is demonstrated in the next screenshot:

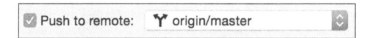

The other way around, which means receiving updates from the server, is called *pull*. To do a pull from the server, you just need to press the *command + option + X* combination key.

Testing with Playground

Playground is a new Xcode 6 feature that allows the programmer to see the Swift code result before it is added to the project. This way, you can test your code separately from the project, receive real-time execution and feedback, and apply it when you are really convinced.

You can use Playground as if it were a separate project by navigating to **File | New | Playground...**. This way, you can do your tests without saving it with the rest of the project.

The other use of Playground is to add it to your project, so you can save your tests with your project. To do this, just add a new file with *command + N*, select the iOS **Source** section, and select **Playground**, as shown in the following screenshot:

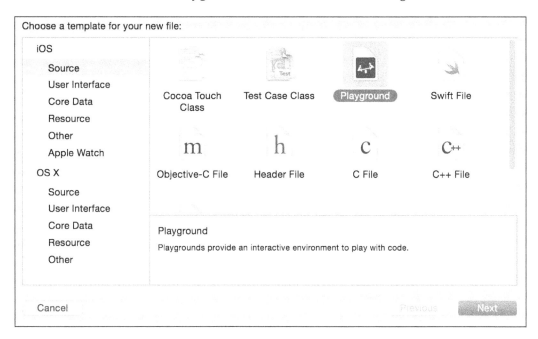

Even if Playground is inside your project or workspace, it won't be able to use your project classes. It means that you might have to copy some files into your Playground and be aware of the modifications, as they are considered to be different containers with their own dependencies.

 Don't use Playground to benchmark or test sensors. It wasn't done for this purpose.

Let's make a sample to create a customized view with Playground. We will create a class called `CustomView`, which inherits from `UIView`. Add a yellow background and a red border. Place the following code to start testing with Playground:

```
class CustomView: UIView {
    override init(frame: CGRect) {
        super.init(frame: frame)

        self.layer.borderColor = UIColor.redColor().CGColor
```

```
            self.backgroundColor = UIColor.yellowColor()
        }

        required init(coder aDecoder: NSCoder) {
            fatalError("init(coder:) has not been implemented")
        }
    }
```

Just below the code, you can create a frame and instantiate it:

```
    var frame = CGRectMake(0, 0, 100, 100)
    var myView = CustomView(frame: frame)
```

On the right-hand side, you will see the word **CustomView** appear. Move the mouse over this word and you will see two small icons appear. One of them is an eye called Quick Look. If you click on it, an image of your view will be displayed, as you can see in the following screenshot:

Here, for example, we can see that something is missing: the red border! The reason is that we are yet to set its width. Let's return to the initializer and add a border to our view:

```
            super.init(frame: frame)
            self.layer.borderWidth = 2
            self.layer.borderColor = UIColor.redColor().CGColor
```

Downloading the example code

You can download the example code files from your account at http://www.packtpub.com for all the Packt Publishing books you have purchased. If you purchased this book elsewhere, you can visit http://www.packtpub.com/support and register to have the files e-mailed directly to you.

Now, you can check your view again using Quick Look. But if you want to get faster results, you can click on the circle icon that is to the right of the Quick Look icon. You will see your square under its declaration. Have a look at the following screenshot to see the expected result:

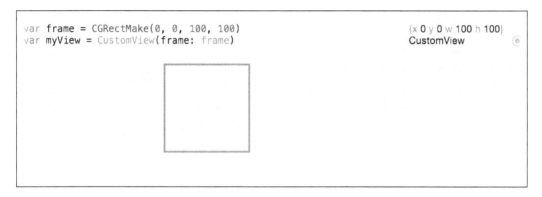

Let's make another change and see how fast Playground gives us results. Add a round corner to your view with the following code:

```
self.layer.cornerRadius = 15
```

As you could see, the Playground took approximately 1 second, as it needs to recompile the code, execute it, and retrieve the result. Don't think about what the sample does by itself. What you do have to think about is how much time you expend testing it on an app every time you have a change and how much time you expend testing it on Playground.

 For more information on how to use Playground, you can read *Swift Cookbook* by Packt Publishing.

Debugging

Debugging is an everyday task for a developer that is usually done to fix a bug. There is no right or wrong way for debugging, and there is no formula to find where the issue is. On the other hand, we have some tricks that can help us find where the bug is. In this section, you are going to see some of them. They can be very useful if you would like to modify any app in this book and you don't get the expected result.

First of all, let's see a common problem. Swift was created to be compatible with Objective-C and Objective-C in its early days was created to be some kind of Smalltalk over the C layer. The idea at that time was to create a language where containers and functions didn't need to be of only a specific type like an array of integers, even the value returned from a function could be of any type. You can see, for example, `NSArray`, `NSDictionary`, and `NSSet` that can store `NSString`, `NSNumber`, and the objects of any other class in the same container.

How Swift receives this kind of information? One way is by using generics but, usually, they are received as `AnyObject`. Sometimes, the debugger is not able to show you the right variable type. For a better example, have a look at the following code:

```
var request = NSURLRequest(URL: NSURL(string:
"http://date.jsontest.com/")!)
NSURLSession.sharedSession().dataTaskWithRequest(request) { (data,
response, error) -> Void in
    var json = NSJSONSerialization.JSONObjectWithData(data,
    options: .MutableContainers, error: nil)
    // json Type???
}.resume()
```

In this case, you can ask yourself what is the JSON variable type? Of course, the first step is to check the debugger information, but you might get some information like the following one:

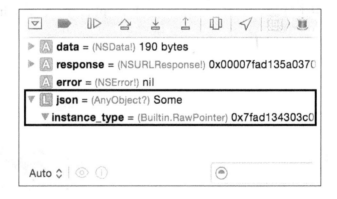

You can check with the `is` operator like `if json is Int`, but it can be very exhausting and, sometimes, even impossible. For scenarios like this, you can use the `_stdlib_getDemangledTypeName` function, which displays the variable type name. In this case, we can add the following `println` instruction to our code, as it is shown in the next code:

```
    var json = NSJSONSerialization.JSONObjectWithData(data,
    options: .MutableContainers, error: nil)
    println("json variable type: \(
    _stdlib_getDemangledTypeName(json!) )")
}.resume()
```

Now, you can see on the log console that, in this case, it is a dictionary as follows:

```
json variable type: __NSDictionaryM
(lldb)
```

In Swift 2, many functions have changed their input or output header from `AnyObject` to a specific type, making life easier for developers.

Another important thing to bear in mind is **lldb**, which is the debugger command line. It can look complex and not much intuitive, but when you get used to it, it is very useful and logical. For example, you can set breakpoints using a pattern like `br s -r viewDid*` to add breakpoints in functions like `viewDidLoad` and `viewDidAppear`.

Of course, there are tasks that you can do with lldb and also with Xcode like using the lldb command `po [[UIWindow keyWindow] recursiveDescription]`, which gives you the window view hierarchy, or simply using the new Debug View Hierarchy button (displayed next) that comes since Xcode 6, which gives you 3D information on the current view.

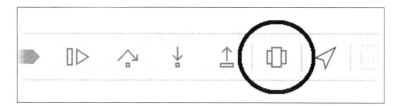

Once it is pressed, you can rotate the image and have an output similar to the following screenshot:

A very common problem in our apps is the excess of memory usage. When we start receiving memory warnings, we need to check the amount of memory that is being increased in some parts of our code. To do it, just keep a function to retrieve the memory whenever you want. The following code is valid to retrieve the amount of memory that is being consumed:

```
func getMemoryUsage() -> mach_vm_size_t{
    let MACH_TASK_BASIC_INFO_COUNT =
    sizeof(mach_task_basic_info_data_t) / sizeof(natural_t)

    let flavor = task_flavor_t(MACH_TASK_BASIC_INFO)
    var size   =
    mach_msg_type_number_t(MACH_TASK_BASIC_INFO_COUNT)
    var pointer =
    UnsafeMutablePointer<mach_task_basic_info>.alloc(1)
    let kerr = task_info(mach_task_self_, flavor,
    UnsafeMutablePointer(pointer), &size)
    let info = pointer.move()

    pointer.dealloc(1)

    if kerr == KERN_SUCCESS {
        return info.resident_size
    } else {
        let message = String(CString: mach_error_string(kerr),
        encoding: NSASCIIStringEncoding)!
        fatalError(message)
    }
}
```

Then, call this function in some parts of your code where you think there is memory wastage and print it like the following code:

```
println("File: \(__FILE__) at line \(__LINE__) memory usage
\(getMemoryUsage())")
```

 There are third-party products that can also help you to debug your app like Fabric (http://www.fabric.io) that sends reports on user crashes to the developer.

New Swift features

Swift is a new language, but it has been changed a few times. While this book was being written, Swift had passed through the 1.2 and 2.0 versions. These versions have some syntax differences compared to the previous ones.

Before the Swift 1.2 version, you couldn't use more than one `let` statement on an `if` statement, so you probably had to write codes like the following one:

```
if let name = product.name {
  if let category = product.category{
    if let price = product.price {
      if price >= 0 {
        println("The product is valid")
      }
    }
  }
}
```

Now, you can reduce the number of lines and write a code like the next one:

```
if let name = product.name,
category = product.category,
price = product.price where price >= 0 {
  println("The product is valid")
}
```

Constants can be initialized after their declaration and before using them, like the following code:

```
let discount:Double
if onSale {
  discount = 0.2
}else {
  discount = 0
}
```

Downcasts and casts that don't return options must use the `as!` operator instead of the old `as` operator. It means that the casting from typical functions that return `AnyObject` must use the new operator. For example, the call to retrieve the index paths of a table view will be as follows:

```
var paths = tableView.indexPathsForRowsInRect(rect) as!
[NSIndexPath]
```

If you have a huge project done with the first Swift version, you might be scared about the number of errors you have for small things like using the new `as!` operator. Fortunately, there is an option to update our Swift code in the **Edit** menu in order to convert our code to the latest Swift version syntax, as it is demonstrated in the following screenshot:

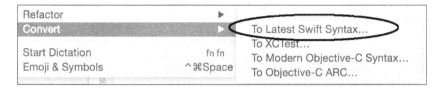

When Swift was announced, it brought with itself new data types that replaced the equivalent Objective-C containers, such as Array for `NSArray`, String to replace `NSString`, and Dictionary for `NSDictionary`, but there was a missing type: `NSSet`. Now, there is `Set` that follows the same rule as its colleagues: it must specify the data type that it will store (generics) and it is interchangeable with `NSSet`.

A new attribute was introduced in the Swift language, it is called `final`. If you have a final class, no class can inherit from it. If you have an attribute or a method, you can't override it.

Some final comments

Working with someone else's code might be a difficult task; you have to figure out what is the logic of the previous developer and how you could change the code to fix a bug, for example. This is the reason why developers must think like a team, act as a team, and work in a team. What does this mean? As a part of our tasks, we should help the next developer by adding comments for them. Swift has its own features based on comments.

Firstly, an interesting part is that Swift allows nested multiline comments. It means that a comment like the following one is not going to stop before `println` like the other languages do:

```
/*
  This code was removed due to it is a bit buggy
  /*
    for i in myArray {
      object.process(i)
    }
  */
  println(myObject.description)
*/
```

Another good thing that we could do with comments is to mark the current state of development. This is equivalent to the #pragma preprocessor in Objective-C. Let's start with // MARK: -, this allows us to add a title before each section of our class. For example, imagine that we have a big class, so we can use this mark to show which methods belong to the base class, which ones belong to the delegates, and which ones are private methods. In this case, we would have a code similar to the following one:

```
// MARK: - Overriden functions
override func viewDidLoad() {
  super.viewDidLoad()
   //…
}
// continue overriding some methods
// MARK: - Delegates
func tableView(tableView: UITableView, willDisplayCell cell:
UITableViewCell, forRowAtIndexPath indexPath: NSIndexPath){
//…
}
// continue writing some delegates methods
// MARK: - private methods
private func createTitle(cellNumber: Int) -> String {
//…
```

In this case, when you click on the editor's combo box (or press *control* + *6* as we learned before), you might see a combo similar to the following screenshot:

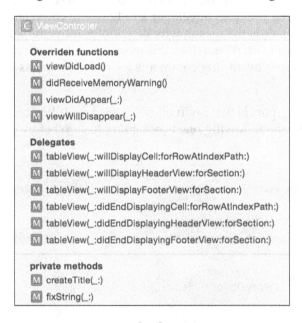

This kind of mark can also be used to reach a differentiated code (something you might check frequently) but, in this case, it is recommended to use it without the dash character, something like `// MARK: Important code`, and it can be done anywhere, even in half a function. Removing the dash from `// MARK:` removes the dividing line in the combo box.

When you have an incomplete code or task, you can mark it with `// TODO:`, meaning that something is pending in this area. For example, imagine that there is a code that is hardcoded and it is desired to load the information from a configuration file. You might have a code similar to the following:

```
// TODO: Retrieve this IP address from the configuration file
return "192.168.20.21"
```

The next mark we have is `// FIXME:`, it represents that this part of the code has a known issue and it should be fixed. Something like the following:

```
// FIXME: The app hangs when there is not internet connection
myconnection.retrieveInformationFromServer()
```

Try to search for `TODO:` and `FIXME:` frequently or do a script that searches for them. There are times when there are too many codes to fix and nobody cares about it.

While you finish this part, don't forget that a well-documented code is a helpful code. When you hold the *option* key and click over a symbol, you will see some information on that symbol, like the `NSURLRequest` box shown in the following screenshot:

24	`var request = NSURLRequest()`
Declaration	`class NSURLRequest : NSObject, NSSecureCoding, NSCoding, NSCopying, NSMutableCopying`
Description	NSURLRequest objects represent a URL load request in a manner independent of protocol and URL scheme.
Availability	iOS (8.0 and later)
Declared In	Foundation
Reference	NSURLRequest Class Reference

You can display equivalent information from your classes, methods, and properties by using `HereDoc`. The idea is very simple; you can take advantage of the comments by starting with `///`, followed by its description as follows:

```
/// A class that represents a garage with its cars
class Garage {
```

Of course, this format is fine when the description is short. However, if you need to write a more exhaustive description, you'd better use the multiline comments starting with /** and closing it with */.

You can also describe the arguments and the value returned with :param: and :returns: as shown in the following code:

```
/**
    Sell a product and remove it from the current stock.

    Remember that:

    - The product must be available
    - the quantity can't be 0 or negative

    :param: product The product you are selling
    :param: quantity Number of units or kilos to sell
    :returns: if the purchase was done correctly
*/
func sellProduct (product: Product, quantity: Int) -> Bool{
```

For example, this code will generate the following box:

27	func sellProduct (product: Product, quantity: Int) -> Bool{
Declaration	func sellProduct(product: Product, quantity: Int) -> Bool
Description	Sell a product and remove it from the current stock.
	Remember that:
	• The product must be available • the quantity can't be 0 or negative
Parameters	product The product you are selling
	quantity Number of units or kilos to sell
Returns	if the purchase was done correctly
Declared In	POS.swift

 You can check for more information on HereDoc at https:// developer.apple.com/library/mac/documentation/ DeveloperTools/Conceptual/HeaderDoc/intro/intro. html#//apple_ref/doc/uid/TP40001215-CH345-SW1.

Summary

In this introductory chapter, we discussed about the basics of Xcode. You learned important keyboard shortcuts that helped us speed up the development. You learned how to set up a project and how to work with this IDE like testing with Playground and using the Git version control.

In the next chapter, we are going to start our first app from scratch. You will learn some of the basic features of the Swift programming language.

2
Creating a City Information App with Customized Table Views

If you've ever developed an app for iOS, you've probably already used a table view. However, you might not have developed it with customized table views or used alternatives for it like the collection view or the page view controller.

Let's start with a simple but a very good app to warm up the engines and learn different ways of displaying collected information with Swift.

In this chapter, we will cover the following:

- Using table view and custom table view cells
- The usage of `UIPageViewController`
- The usage of `UICollectionViewController`
- The usage of external APIs
- Managing JSON messages
- The usage of `NSURLSession` to receive JSON or download pictures
- Custom `NSErrors`

Project overview

The idea of this app is to give users information about cities such as the current weather, pictures, history, and cities that are around.

How can we do it? Firstly, we have to decide on how the app is going to suggest a city to the user. Of course, the most logical city would be the city where the user is located, which means that we have to use the **Core Location** framework to retrieve the device's coordinates with the help of GPS.

Once we have retrieved the user's location, we can search for cities next to it. To do this, we are going to use a service from http://www.geonames.org/.

Another piece of information that will be necessary is the weather. Of course, there are a lot of websites that can give us information on the weather forecast, but not all of them offer an API to use it for your app. In this case, we are going to use the **Open Weather Map** service.

What about pictures? For pictures, we can use the famous Flickr. Easy, isn't it? Now that we have the necessary information, let's start with our app.

Setting it up

Before we start coding, we are going to register the needed services and create an empty app. First, let's create a user at geonames. Just go to http://www.geonames.org/login with your favorite browser, sign up as a new user, and confirm it when you receive a confirmation e-mail. It may seem that everything has been done, however, you still need to upgrade your account to use the API services. Don't worry, it's free! So, open http://www.geonames.org/manageaccount and upgrade your account.

 Don't use the user *demo* provided by geonames, even for development. This user exceeds its daily quota very frequently.

With geonames, we can receive information on cities by their coordinates, but we don't have the weather forecast and pictures. For weather forecasts, open http://openweathermap.org/register and register a new user and API.

Lastly, we need a service for the cities' pictures. In this case, we are going to use Flickr. Just create a Yahoo! account and create an API key at https://www.flickr.com/services/apps/create/.

While creating a new app, try to investigate the services available for it and their current status. Unfortunately, the APIs change a lot like their prices, their terms, and even their features.

The API keys used in this book are fake, please replace them with the corresponding API key given to you by the service provider.

Now, we can start creating the app. Open Xcode, create a new single view application for iOS, and call it Chapter 2 City Info. Make sure that **Swift** is the main language as shown in the following screenshot:

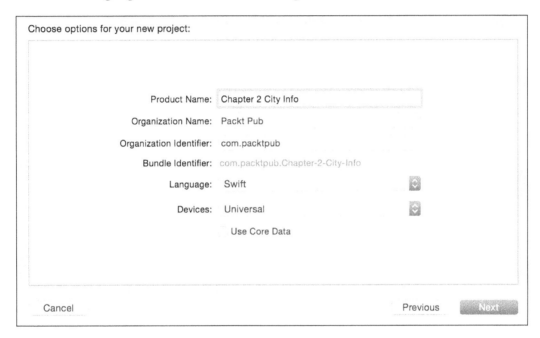

The first task here is to add a library to help us work with JSON messages. In this case, a library called SwiftyJSON will solve our problem. Otherwise, it would be hard work to navigate through the NSJSONSerialization results.

Download the SwiftyJSON library from https://github.com/SwiftyJSON/ SwiftyJSON/archive/master.zip, then uncompress it, and copy the SwiftyJSON. swift file in your project.

Another very common way of installing third-party libraries or frameworks would be to use **CocoaPods**, which is commonly known as just **PODs**. This is a dependency manager, which downloads the desired frameworks with their dependencies and updates them. Check https://cocoapods.org/ for more information.

Ok, so now it is time to start coding. We will create some functions and classes that should be common for the whole program. As you know, many functions return NSError if something goes wrong. However, sometimes, there are errors that are detected by the code, like when you receive a JSON message with an unexpected struct. For this reason, we are going to create a class that creates custom NSError. Once we have it, we will add a new file to the project (*command* + *N*) called ErrorFactory.swift and add the following code:

```swift
import Foundation
class ErrorFactory {{
    static let Domain = "CityInfo"
    enum Code:Int {
        case WrongHttpCode = 100,
        MissingParams = 101,
        AuthDenied = 102,
        WrongInput = 103
    }

    class func error(code:Code) -> NSError{
        let description:String
        let reason:String
        let recovery:String
        switch code {
        case .WrongHttpCode:
            description = NSLocalizedString("Server replied wrong
            code (not 200, 201 or 304)", comment: "")
            reason = NSLocalizedString("Wrong server or wrong
            api", comment: "")
            recovery =  NSLocalizedString("Check if the server is
            is right one", comment: "")
        case .MissingParams:
            description = NSLocalizedString("There are some
            missing params", comment: "")
            reason =  NSLocalizedString("Wrong endpoint or API
            version", comment: "")
            recovery = NSLocalizedString("Check the url and the
            server version", comment: "")
        case .AuthDenied:
```

```
            description = NSLocalizedString("Authorization
            denied", comment: "")
            reason =  NSLocalizedString("User must accept the
            authorization for using its feature", comment: "")
            recovery = NSLocalizedString("Open user auth panel.",
            comment: "")
        case .WrongInput:
            description = NSLocalizedString("A parameter was
            wrong", comment: "")
            reason = NSLocalizedString("Probably a cast wasn't
            correct", comment: "")
            recovery = NSLocalizedString("Check the input
            parameters.", comment: "")
        }
        return NSError(domain: ErrorFactory.Domain, code:
        code.rawValue, userInfo: [
            NSLocalizedDescriptionKey: description,
            NSLocalizedFailureReasonErrorKey: reason,
            NSLocalizedRecoverySuggestionErrorKey: recovery
            ])
    }
}
```

The previous code shows the usage of NSError that requires a domain, which is a string that differentiates the error type/origin and avoids collisions in the error code.

The error code is just an integer that represents the error that occurred. We used an enumeration based on integer values, which makes it easier for the developer to remember and allows us to convert its enumeration to an integer easily with the rawValue property.

The third argument of an NSError initializer is a dictionary that contains messages, which can be useful to the user (actually to the developer). Here, we have three keys:

- NSLocalizedDescriptionKey: This contains a basic description of the error
- NSLocalizedFailureReasonErrorKey: This explains what caused the error
- NSLocalizedRecoverySuggestionErrorKey: This shows what is possible to avoid this error

As you might have noticed, for these strings, we used a function called NSLocalizedString, which will retrieve the message in the corresponding language if it is set to the Localizable.strings file.

So, let's add a new file to our app and call it `Helpers.swift`; click on it for editing. URLs have special character combinations that represent special characters, for example, a whitespace in a URL is sent as a combination of 20% and a open parenthesis is sent with the combination of 28%. The `stringByAddingPercentEncodingWithAllowedCharacters` string method allows us to do this character conversion.

> If you need more information on the percent encoding, you can check the Wikipedia entry at https://en.wikipedia.org/wiki/Percent-encoding. As we are going to work with web APIs, we will need to encode some texts before we send them to the corresponding server.

Type the following function to convert a dictionary into a string with the URL encoding:

```
func toUriEncoded(params: [String:String]) -> String {
    var records = [String]()
    for (key, value) in params {
        let valueEncoded = value.
stringByAddingPercentEncodingWithAllowedCharacters(.
URLHostAllowedCharacterSet())
        records.append("\(key)=\(valueEncoded!)")
    }
    return "&".join(records)
}
```

Another common task is to call the main queue. You might have already used a code like `dispatch_async(dispatch_get_main_queue(), {() -> () in ... })`, however, it is too long. We can reduce it by calling it something like M{...}. So, here is the function for it:

```
func M(((completion: () -> () ) {
    dispatch_async(dispatch_get_main_queue(), completion)
}
```

A common task is to request for JSON messages. To do so, we just need to know the endpoint, the required parameters, and the callback. So, we can start with this function as follows:

```
func requestJSON(urlString:String, params:[String:String] = [:],
completion:(JSON, NSError?) -> Void){
    let fullUrlString = "\(urlString)?\(toUriEncoded(params))"
    if let url = NSURL(string: fullUrlString) {
        NSURLSession.sharedSession().dataTaskWithURL(url) { (data,
        response, error) -> Void in
```

```
if error != nil {
    completion(JSON(NSNull()), error)
    return
}

var jsonData = data!
var jsonString = NSString(data: jsonData, encoding:
NSUTF8StringEncoding)!
```

Here, we have to add a tricky code, because the Flickr API is always returned with a callback function called `jsonFlickrApi` while wrapping the corresponding JSON. This callback must be removed before the JSON text is parsed. So, we can fix this issue by adding the following code:

```
// if it is the Flickr response we have to remove the
callback function jsonFlickrApi()
// from the JSON string
if (jsonString as
String).characters.startsWith("jsonFlickrApi(".characters)
{
        jsonString =
jsonString.substringFromIndex("jsonFlickrApi(".characters.count)
        let end = (jsonString as String).characters.count - 1
        jsonString = jsonString.substringToIndex(end)
        jsonData =
jsonString.dataUsingEncoding(NSUTF8StringEncoding)!
        }
```

Now, we can complete this function by creating a JSON object and calling the callback:

```
let json = JSON(data:jsonData)
completion(json, nil)

}.resume()
}else {
    completion(JSON(NSNull()),
    ErrorFactory.error(.WrongInput))
}
}
```

At this point, the app has a good skeleton. It means that, from now on, we can code the app itself.

The first scene

Create a project group (*command* + *option* + *N*) for the view controllers and move the `ViewController.swift` file (created by Xcode) to this group. As we are going to have more than one view controller, it would also be a good idea to rename it to `InitialViewController.swift`:

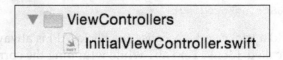

Now, open this file and rename its class from `ViewController` to `InitialViewController`:

    class **InitialViewController**: UIViewController {

Once the class is renamed, we need to update the corresponding view controller in the storyboard by:

- Clicking on the storyboard.
- Selecting the view controller (the only one we have till now).
- Going to the Identity inspector by using the *command* + *option* + *3* combination. Here, you can update the class name to the new one.
- Pressing enter and confirming that the module name is automatically updated from **None** to the product name.

The following picture demonstrates where you should do this change and how it should be after the change:

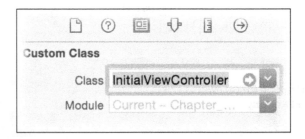

Great! Now, we can draw the scene. Firstly, let's change the view background color. To do it, select the view that hangs from the view controller. Go to the **Attribute Inspector** by pressing *command + option + 4*, look for background color, and choose other, as shown in the following picture:

When the color dialog appears, choose the Color Sliders option at the top and select the **RGB Sliders** combo box option. Then, you can change the color as per your choice. In this case, let's set it to 250 for the three colors:

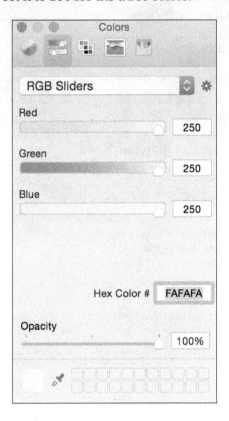

 Before you start a new app, create a mockup of every scene. In this mockup, try to write down the color numbers for the backgrounds, fonts, and so on. Remember that Xcode still doesn't have a way to work with styles as websites do with CSS, meaning that if you have to change the default background color, for example, you will have to repeat it everywhere.

On the storyboard's right-hand side, you have the Object Library, which can be easily accessed with the *command + option + control + 3* combination. From there, you can search for views, view controllers, and gestures, and drag them to the storyboard or scene. The following picture shows a sample of it:

Now, add two labels, a search bar, and a table view. The first label should be the app title, so let's write City Info on it. Change its alignment to center, the font to **American Typewriter**, and the font size to **24**.

On the other label, let's do the same, but write `Please select your city` and its font size should be **18**. The scene must result in something similar to the following picture:

Do we still need to do anything else on this storyboard scene? The answer is yes. Now it is time for the auto layout, otherwise the scene components will be misplaced when you start the app.

There are different ways to add auto layout constraints to a component. An easy way of doing it is by selecting the component by clicking on it like the top label. With the *control* key pressed, drag it to the other component on which the constraint will be based like the main view. The following picture shows a sample of a constraint being created from a table to the main view:

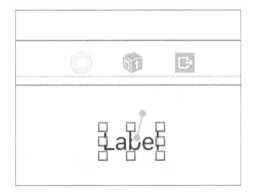

Another way is by selecting the component and clicking on the left or on the middle button, which are to the bottom-right of the interface builder screen. The following picture highlights these buttons:

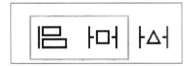

Whatever is your favorite way of adding constraints, you will need the following constraints and values for the current scene:

- City Info label center X equals to the center of superview (main view), value 0
- City Info label top equals to the top layout guide, value 0
- Select your city label top vertical spacing of 8 to the City Info label
- Select your city label alignment center X to superview, value 0
- Search bar top value 8 to select your city label
- Search bar trailing and leading space 0 to superview
- Table view top space (space 0) to the search bar
- Table view trailing and leading space 0 to the search bar
- Table view bottom 0 to superview

Before continuing, it is a good idea to check whether the layout suits for every resolution. To do it, open the assistant editor with *command + option + .return* and change its view to **Preview**:

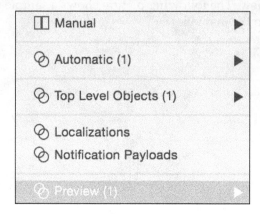

Here, you can have a preview of your screen on the device. You can also rotate the screens by clicking on the icon with a square and a arched arrow over it:

Click on the plus sign to the bottom-left of the assistant editor to add more screens:

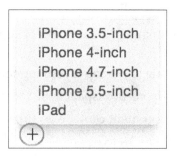

Once you are happy with your layout, you can move on to the next step. Although the storyboard is not yet done, we are going to leave it for a while.

Click on the `InitialViewController.swift` file. Let's start receiving information on where the device is using the GPS. To do it, import the Core Location framework and set the view controller as a delegate:

```
import CoreLocation

class InitialViewController: UIViewController,
CLLocationManagerDelegate {
```

After this, we can set the core location manager as a property and initialize it on `viewDidLoadMethod`. Type the following code to set `locationManager` and initialize `InitialViewController`:

```
var locationManager = CLLocationManager()

override func viewDidLoad() {
    super.viewDidLoad()
    locationManager.delegate = self
    locationManager.desiredAccuracy =
    kCLLocationAccuracyThreeKilometers
    locationManager.distanceFilter = 3000
    if
locationManager.respondsToSelector(Selector("requestWhenInUseAuthoriz
ation")) {
        locationManager.requestWhenInUseAuthorization()
    }
    locationManager.startUpdatingLocation()
}
```

After initializing the location manager, we have to check whether the GPS is working or not by implementing the `didUpdateLocations` method. Right now, we are going to print the last location and nothing more:

```
func locationManager(manager: CLLocationManager!,
didUpdateLocations locations: [CLLocation]!){
    let lastLocation = locations.last!
    print(lastLocation)
}
```

Now, we can test the app. However, we still need to perform one more step. Go to your `Info.plist` file by pressing *command + option + J* and the file name. Add a new entry with the `NSLocationWhenInUseUsageDescription` key and change its type to **String** and its value to **This app needs to know your location**.

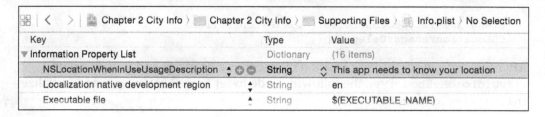

This last step is mandatory since iOS 8. Press play and check whether you have received a coordinate, but not very frequently.

Displaying the cities' information

The next step is to create a class to store the information received from the Internet. In this case, we can do it in a straightforward manner by copying the JSON object properties in our class properties. Create a new group called `Models` and, inside it, a file called `CityInfo.swift`. There you can code `CityInfo` as follows:

```
class CityInfo {
    var fcodeName:String?
    var wikipedia:String?
    var geonameId: Int!
    var population:Int?
    var countrycode:String?
    var fclName:String?
    var lat : Double!
    var lng: Double!
    var fcode: String?
    var toponymName:String?
    var name:String!
    var fcl:String?

    init?(json:JSON){){){
        // if any required field is missing we must not create the
        object.
        if let name = json["name"].string,,, geonameId =
        json["geonameId"].int, lat = json["lat"].double,
            lng = json["lng"].double {
            self.name = name
```

```
            self.geonameId = geonameId
            self.lat = lat
            self.lng = lng
        }else{
            return nil
        }

        self.fcodeName = json["fcodeName"].string
        self.wikipedia = json["wikipedia"].string
        self.population = json["population"].int
        self.countrycode = json["countrycode"].string
        self.fclName = json["fclName"].string
        self.fcode = json["fcode"].string
        self.toponymName = json["toponymName"].string
        self.fcl = json["fcl"].string
    }
}
```

Pay attention that our initializer has a question mark on its header; this is called a **failable initializer**. Traditional initializers always return a new instance of the newly requested object. However, with failable initializers, you can return a new instance or a nil value, indicating that the object couldn't be constructed.

In this initializer, we used an object of the JSON type, which is a class that belongs to the SwiftyJSON library/framework. You can easily access its members by using brackets with string indices to access the members of a json object, like json ["field name"], or using brackets with integer indices to access elements of a json array.

Doesn't matter, the way you have to use the return type, it will always be a JSON object, which can't be directly assigned to the variables of another built-in types, such as integers, strings, and so on. Casting from a JSON object to a basic type can be done by accessing properties with the same name as the destination type, such as .string for casting to string objects, .int for casting to int objects, .array or an array of JSON objects, and so on.

Now, we have to think about how this information is going to be displayed. As we have to display this information repeatedly, a good way to do so would be with a table view. Therefore, we will create a custom table view cell for it.

Go to your project navigator, create a new group called `Cells`, and add a new file called `CityInfoCell.swift`. Here, we are going to implement a class that inherits from `UITableViewCell`. Note that the whole object can be configured just by setting the `cityInfo` property:

```swift
import UIKit

class CityInfoCell:UITableViewCell {
    @IBOutlet var nameLabel:UILabel!
    @IBOutlet var coordinates:UILabel!
    @IBOutlet var population:UILabel!
    @IBOutlet var infoImage:UIImageView!

    private var _cityInfo:CityInfo!
    var cityInfo:CityInfo {
        get {
            return _cityInfo
        }
        set (cityInfo){
            self._cityInfo = cityInfo
            self.nameLabel.text = cityInfo.name
            if let population = cityInfo.population {
                self.population.text = "Pop: \(population)"
            }else {
                self.population.text = ""
            }

            self.coordinates.text = String(format: "%.02f, %.02f",
            cityInfo.lat, cityInfo.lng)

            if let _ = cityInfo.wikipedia  {
                self.infoImage.image = UIImage(named: "info")
            }
        }
    }
}
```

Return to the storyboard and add a table view cell from the object library to the table view by dragging it. Click on this table view cell and add three labels and one image view to it. Try to organize it with something similar to the following picture:

Change the labels font family to **American Typewriter**, and the font size to 16 for the city name and 12 for the population and the location label. The image on the left-hand side for the image view can be downloaded from this book's resources. Drag the info.png and noinfo.png images to your Images.xcassets project. Go back to your storyboard and set the image to noinfo in the UIImageView attribute inspector, as shown in the following screenshot:

As you know, we have to set the auto layout constraints. Just remember that the constraints will take the table view cell as superview. So, here you have the constraints that need to be set:

- City name label leading equals 0 to the leading margin (left)
- City name label top equals 0 to the super view top margin
- City name label bottom equals 0 to the super view bottom margin
- City label horizontal space 8 to the population label
- Population leading equals 0 to the superview center X
- Population top equals to -8 to the superview top
- Population trailing (right) equals 8 to the noinfo image
- Population bottom equals 0 to the location top
- Population leading equals 0 to the location leading
- Location height equals to 21

- Location trailing equals 8 to the image leading
- Location bottom equals 0 to the image bottom
- Image trailing equals 0 to the superview trailing margin
- Image aspect ratio width equals 0 to the image height
- Image bottom equals -8 to the superview bottom
- Image top equals -8 to the superview top

Has everything been done for this table view cell? Of course not. We still need to set its class and connect each component. Select the table view cell and change its class to `CityInfoCell`:

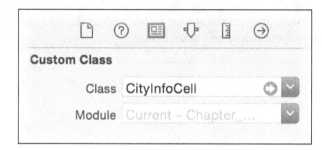

As we are here, let's do a similar task that is to change the cell identifier to `cityinfocell`. This way, we can easily instantiate the cell from our code:

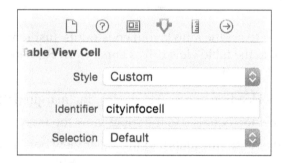

Now, you can connect the cell components with the ones we have in the `CityInfoCell` class and also connect the table view with the view controller:

```
@IBOutlet var tableView: UITableView!!
```

There are different ways to connect a view with the corresponding property. An easy way is to open the assistant view with the *command + option + enter* combination, leaving the storyboard on the left-hand side and the Swift file on the right-hand side. Then, you just need to drag the circle that will appear on the left-hand side of the @IBOutlet or the @IBAction attribute and connect with the corresponding visual object on the storyboard.

After this, we need to set the table view delegate and data source, and also the search bar delegate with the view controller. It means that the InitialViewController class needs to have the following header. Replace the current InitialViewController header with:

```
class InitialViewController: UIViewController,
CLLocationManagerDelegate, UITableViewDataSource,
UITableViewDelegate, UISearchBarDelegate {
```

Connect the table view and search bar delegate and the data source with the view controller by control dragging from the table view to the view controller's icon at the top of the screen, as shown in the following screenshot:

Coding the initial view controller

The InitialViewController class will display the possible cities where the user is located. Let's continue with the InitialViewController class and complete its code. To complete this code, we need to think about where we are going to store the received information. We will need two arrays of CityInfo: one is to store every object received from the server and the other is to store the objects that are shown after the user's filter. These arrays must be stored as properties:

```
private var cities = [CityInfo]()
private var citiesDisplayed = [CityInfo]()
```

At this point, we can complete the `didUpdateLocations` method, which belongs to the `CLLocationManagerDelegate` protocol. Now, we can request information of the cities that are around us. Type the following code to implement the `didUpdateLocations` method, replacing the `yourgeonamesuser` word with the username you registered on geonames:

```
func locationManager(manager: CLLocationManager!,
didUpdateLocations locations: [CLLocation]!){
    let lastLocation = locations.last!
    print(lastLocation)
    let accurrancy = 0.2
    requestJSON("http://api.geonames.org/citiesJSON", params:
    [
        "north":"\(lastLocation.coordinate.latitude +
        accurrancy)",
        "south":"\(lastLocation.coordinate.latitude -
        accurrancy)",
        "east":"\(lastLocation.coordinate.longitude +
        accurrancy)",
        "west":"\(lastLocation.coordinate.longitude -
        accurrancy)",
        "lang":"en",
        "username":"yourgeonamesuser"" // replace
        yourgeonameuser with the username you registered on
        geonames.
    ]) { (json, error) -> Void in
        if error != nil {
            print(error?.localizedDescription)
            return
        }
        if let status = json["status"].dictionary {
            print("Error")
        }else if let cities = json["geonames"].array {
            self.citiesDisplayed = [CityInfo]()
            self.cities = cities.reduce([CityInfo]()) {
            (citiesInfo, json) -> [CityInfo] in
                var citiesCopy = citiesInfo
                if let cityInfo = CityInfo(json: json) {
                    citiesCopy.append(cityInfo)
                    self.citiesDisplayed.append(cityInfo)
                }
                return citiesCopy
            }

            M {
```

```
                    self.tableView.reloadData()
                }
            }else {
                print("error")
            }
        }
    }
```

As you can imagine, the table view isn't going to display anything if we don't complete the table view data source methods. So, we can just complete the table view data source by adding the following code to our InitialViewController class:

```
// MARK: - TableView Datasource and delegate
func tableView(tableView: UITableView, numberOfRowsInSection
section: Int) -> Int{
    return self.citiesDisplayed.count
}


func tableView(tableView: UITableView, cellForRowAtIndexPath
indexPath: NSIndexPath) -> UITableViewCell{
    let cell =
    tableView.dequeueReusableCellWithIdentifier("cityinfocell")
as!
    CityInfoCell
    cell.cityInfo = self.citiesDisplayed[indexPath.row]
    return cell
}
```

Don't forget that we still have to filter the cities following the information typed in the search bar. It means that we have to implement the searchBar:textDidChange method that belongs to the UISearchBarDelegate protocol with the following code:

```
// MARK: - UISearchBar delegate
func searchBar(searchBar: UISearchBar, textDidChange
searchText: String) {
    self.citiesDisplayed = [CityInfo]()
    for cityInfo in self.cities {
        if searchText == "" {
            citiesDisplayed.append(cityInfo)
        }else if cityInfo.name.lowercaseString.
rangeOfString(searchText.lowercaseString) != nil{
            citiesDisplayed.append(cityInfo)
        }
    }
    self.tableView.reloadData()
}
```

The logic of this code is very easy; we just have to check whether the typed text is found in a record. If so, we have to add it to the `citiesDisplayed` array. An exception is the empty string. In this case, we have to add every record to the array.

 Pay attention that we converted both strings to lowercase to compare them. If you prefer, you can use `cityInfo.name.rangeOfString(searchText, options: .CaseInsensitiveSearch)`.

Rebuild your app and run it to check whether everything is working:

Adding the page view controller

To display the city's information, we are going to use a page view controller. This way, we can navigate through its information as if we were reading a book. To do it, we are going to add a new file called `CityOptionsViewController.swift` to the `ViewControllers` group.

Open this file and create a class that inherits from `UIPageViewController` and also stores `CityInfo`. This class should also be its own data source, as it needs to know which view controller comes next when the user decides to turn a page. As we don't yet have any of the view controllers that are going to hang from this page view controller, we are going to implement the mandatory methods that will return `nil`. Let's start implementing the `CityOptionsViewController` class with a minimum code by typing the following code:

```
import UIKit

class CityOptionsViewController : UIPageViewController,
UIPageViewControllerDataSource {
    var cityInfo:CityInfo!
    override func viewDidLoad() {
        super.viewDidLoad()
        self.dataSource = self
        self.doubleSided = false
    }
    func pageViewController(pageViewController:
UIPageViewController, viewControllerBeforeViewController
viewController: UIViewController) -> UIViewController? {
        return nil
    }
    func pageViewController(pageViewController:
UIPageViewController, viewControllerAfterViewController
viewController: UIViewController) -> UIViewController? {
        return nil
    }
}
```

This code is not finished yet. We will complete it later, when we start creating the view controllers. Return to the storyboard and add a page view controller to it by dragging it from the object library. The following picture shows the page view controller in the object library:

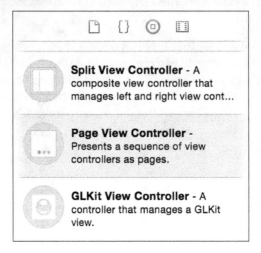

Select the page view controller and go to its Identity inspector by pressing *command + option + 3*. Here, we have to change its class to CityOptionsViewController and the storyboard ID to cityoptions.

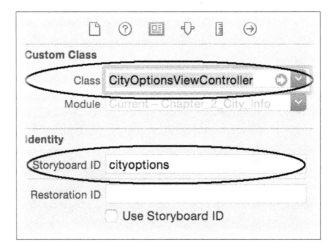

Now, we are able to call this page view controller. All we have to do is to return to `InitialViewController` and add a method that will give the `CityInfo` object to our page view controller and present the new view controller. Remember that this method is called when the user taps on the corresponding table cell, which means that we have to implement the `didSelectRowAtIndexPath` method with this code:

```
func tableView(tableView: UITableView, didSelectRowAtIndexPath
indexPath: NSIndexPath){
    let viewController =
self.storyboard?.instantiateViewControllerWithIdentifier("cityoptio
ns") as! CityOptionsViewController
    viewController.cityInfo =
self.citiesDisplayed[indexPath.row]
    self.presentViewController(viewController, animated: true,
    completion: nil)
}
```

Press play and confirm whether the app is working. When you tap on a city, a black screen will appear.

Displaying the Wikipedia information

Now, we are going to display the city information by displaying its Wikipedia page. To do it, we need to add a new view controller to our app. So, we will add a new Swift file called `WikiViewController.swift` to the `ViewControllers` group.

Right now we are only going to create an almost empty class; nevertheless, we are going to return here after a while to complete its code.

```
import UIKit
class WikiViewController:UIViewController {
    var cityInfo:CityInfo!
}
```

Go back to the storyboard and add a new view controller to it. Open the view controller's Identity inspector, and change its class from the default one to `WikiViewController`. Taking advantage that we are on the Identity inspector, let's also change the **Storyboard ID** to `wikicity` as it is shown in the following screenshot:

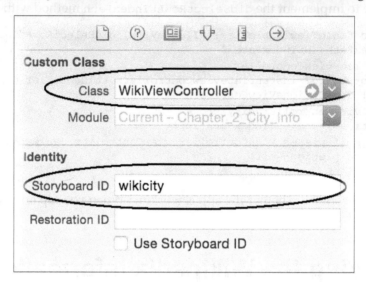

After this, we can change the view background to gray (FAFAFA) and add two labels and a web view to the layout. Write `City Info` on the first label, change its alignment to center and its font to **American Typewriter** with a font size of 24, and place it at the top.

The second label should contain the text **Wiki** with center alignment and an **American Typewriter** font of size 18. Place it under the first label. The web view should take the rest of the view. At this point, you should have a layout similar to the following:

After placing the components in the layout, we have to add the following auto layout constraints:

- City Info label center X equals 0 to superview center X
- City Info label top equals 0 to the top layout guide
- City Info label bottom equals 0 to the Wiki label top
- Wiki label center X equals 0 to the superview center X
- Wiki label bottom equals 0 to the web view top
- Web view bottom equals 0 to the superview layout guide
- Web view trailing equals 0 to the superview trailing margin
- Web view leading equals 0 to the superview leading margin

Once the layout is complete, we can connect the web view with the view controller and implement the `viewDidLoad` method of `WikiViewController`. In this case, we first need to check whether we have the Wikipedia page of the current city to display in the web view. If we don't have the Wikipedia page, we can call the Wikipedia search page. The final code of our class must be as follows:

```
class WikiViewController:UIViewController {
    var cityInfo:CityInfo!
    @IBOutlet var webView: UIWebView!

    override func viewDidLoad() {
        let url:NSURL
        if let wikipediaInfo = self.cityInfo.wikipedia {
            url = NSURL(string: "http://\(wikipediaInfo)")!
        }else {
            url =
NSURL(string:"http://en.wikipedia.org/w/index.php?search=\(self.
cityInfo.name)")!
        }
        let request = NSURLRequest(URL: url)
        self.webView.loadRequest(request)
    }
}
```

> In this case, we didn't implement `UIWebViewDelegate` to detect errors, however, it is a good idea to do it.

Of course, nothing different will happen if we press play. The reason is that we need to add an instance of this view controller to the page view controller. So, we will return to the `CityOptionsViewController` code. First, we add a new array of view controllers as an property. This array will be used to retain the view controllers' instance and to know which view controller would come up when the user turns a page:

```
private var cityViewControllers = [UIViewController]()
```

Then, we can complete the `viewDidLoad` method as we need to instantiate `WikiViewController` and set it as the view controller that is going to be displayed:

```
override func viewDidLoad() {
    super.viewDidLoad()
    self.dataSource = self
```

```
        self.doubleSided = false

        let wikiViewController =
        self.storyboard?.instantiateViewControllerWithIdentifier("wiki
city") as! WikiViewController
        wikiViewController.cityInfo = self.cityInfo
        cityViewControllers.append(wikiViewController)

        self.setViewControllers([wikiViewController], direction:
        .Forward, animated: true) { (_) -> Void in
            return
        }
    }
}
```

Now, we can implement the page view controller data source methods.
Even with only one view controller right now, we must implement it as
a generic one. This way, we don't need to modify them every time we
add a new view controller. We will complete the implementation that
we have till now for the viewControllerBeforeViewController and
viewControllerAfterViewController methods with the following code:

```
    func pageViewController(pageViewController:
    UIPageViewController, viewControllerBeforeViewController
    viewController: UIViewController) -> UIViewController? {
        if let position = cityViewControllers.indexOf(
        viewController) where position > 0{
            return cityViewControllers[position - 1]
        }
        return nil
    }
    func pageViewController(pageViewController:
    UIPageViewController, viewControllerAfterViewController
    viewController: UIViewController) -> UIViewController? {
        if let position = cityViewControllers.indexOf(
        viewController) where position < cityViewControllers.count
        - 1 {
            return cityViewControllers[position + 1]
        }
        return nil
    }
```

Rebuild the app and run it. Check whether, after selecting a city, you are able to see the city's Wikipedia page:

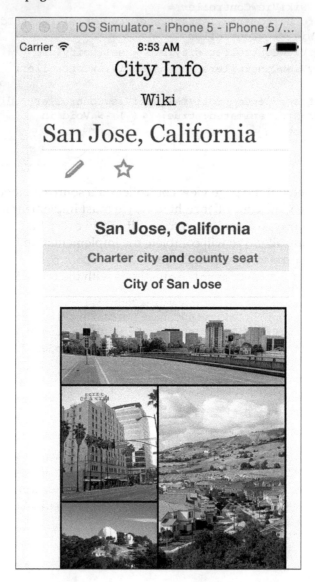

Displaying weather forecasts

Once the user is happy with the city's information, he/she can also retrieve the weather forecast. As it was already mentioned, the weather forecast is going to be retrieved from Open Weather Map instead of geonames.

We just have to think about how this "scene" is going to work. The idea is to display weather information such as the date and time, the temperature, and an icon of the sun if it is during the day time or a moon when the estimated weather is during the night. If the table view cell needs to display rainy weather, we should use another cell template. This one should display the same information as the other cell, but with an exception that the icon will show rain. We are also going to display additional information on the amount of rain.

Once we have the idea clear, we can start implementing the view controller. Select the `ViewControllers` group, add a new file called `WeatherViewController.swift`, and start creating a class with the same name. As we discussed before, the information will be displayed with a table view, so we also need to implement the table view data source protocol:

```
import Foundation
import UIKit

class WeatherViewController:UIViewController,
UITableViewDataSource {
```

As properties, we will need to store the current `CityInfo` object, an array of forecasts for the table view (in this case, each forecast is a JSON object) and, of course, the table view itself to request it to reload the data:

```
var cityInfo:CityInfo!
var forecast = [JSON]()
@IBOutlet var tableView: UITableView!
```

We can request for the forecast records in the `viewDidLoad` method. It should be straightforward, as we just need to request for information, store the information, and ask the table view to reload its data. Type the following `viewDidLoad` implementation to retrieve data from the Open Weather Map site:

```
override func viewDidLoad() {
    requestJSON("http://api.openweathermap.org/data/2.5/forecast",
        params: ["lat": "\(cityInfo.lat)",
            "lon": "\(cityInfo.lng)"]) { (json, error) -> Void
            in
                if error != nil {
                    print(error!.localizedDescription)
                    return
                }
                self.forecast = json["list"].arrayValue
                M {
                    self.tableView.reloadData()
                }
        }
}
```

Now, we just need to implement the table view data source's methods, starting with `numberOfRowsInSection` that should return the forecast array size:

```
func tableView(tableView: UITableView, numberOfRowsInSection
section: Int) -> Int{
    return forecast.count
}
```

The `cellForRowAtIndexPath` method is very similar to the one implemented on `InitialViewController` but, here, we have a small detail. First, we are going to check whether it is rainy and, according to it, we are going to retrieve one cell layout or another. Don't worry about the compilation errors that you are going to receive now, just implement the method and close the class with the following code:

```
func tableView(tableView: UITableView, cellForRowAtIndexPath
indexPath: NSIndexPath) -> UITableViewCell{
    let currentForecast = forecast[indexPath.row]
    var cell:WeatherCell
    if let rain = currentForecast["rain"]["3h"].double where
    rain > 0 {
        cell =
tableView.dequeueReusableCellWithIdentifier("raincell") as!
RainCell

    } else {
        cell =
tableView.dequeueReusableCellWithIdentifier("weathercell") as!
WeatherCell
    }
    cell.setUIFromJSON(currentForecast)
    return cell
}
}
```

As you see, with the compiler's errors, it is still pending to implement two table view cell classes: `WeatherCell` and `RainCell`. Add a new file called `WeatherCell.swift` to the cells group and add the following content:

```
import UIKit

class WeatherCell:UITableViewCell{

    @IBOutlet var tempMax: UILabel!
    @IBOutlet var dateAndTime: UILabel!
```

```
@IBOutlet var icon: UIImageView!

func setUIFromJSON(json:JSON){
    let date = json["dt_txt"].stringValue
    let hour = Int(date.componentsSeparatedByString("
    ")[1].componentsSeparatedByString(":")[0])!
    if hour > 5 && hour < 20 {
        self.icon.image = UIImage(named:"sun")
    } else {
        self.icon.image = UIImage(named:"moon")
    }
    self.tempMax.text = String(format:"%.01fC",
    json["main"]["temp_max"].doubleValue - 272.15)
    self.dateAndTime.text = date
    }
}
```

We still have one compilation error, let's solve it by adding a new file called
`RainCell.swift` to the cells group. Now, we have to implement a class that is
basically the same as the previous one, but by adding new information. Therefore,
we just need to inherit from the previous class and complete it with the new code:

```
import UIKit

class RainCell:WeatherCell {
    @IBOutlet var waterLabel: UILabel!

    override func setUIFromJSON(json:JSON){
        super.setUIFromJSON(json)
        self.icon.image = UIImage(named:"rain")
        self.waterLabel.text = String(format:
        "%.02fmm",json["rain"]["3h"].doubleValue)
    }
}
```

The errors have gone but, if you are a good observer, you might have noticed that we
are loading images that are not yet in our project. Go to the book resources and drag
the `rain.png`, `sun.png` and `moon.png` images into your `images.xcassets` project.

The pictures included in the book resources are in their original size. The
right way of using them is by using three different sizes for each picture.
However, this task should be done with an external program such as
Photoshop and GIMP or by using Vector Graphics if the your original
image is a PDF vector. Both cases are out of the scope of this book.

The coding task for this page is done, so it is time to return to the storyboard. Add a new view controller, select it, and go to its Identity inspector. Change the class name to `WeatherViewController` and its **Storyboard ID** to `weathercity`, as shown in the following picture:

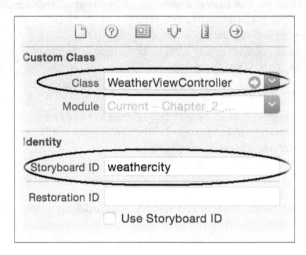

Now, create a layout similar to `InitialViewController`, except that the subtitle label should be **Weather Forecast**. Don't forget to connect the table view with `WeatherViewController` and also set it as the table view's delegate.

Once the layout is ready, you need to add two table view cells to the table view. For the first one, change its class in the Identity inspector to `WeatherCell` and its identifier in the attribute inspector to `weathercell`. The second cell's class should be `RainCell` and its identifier should be `raincell`.

In both the cells, add two labels and a picture on the left-hand side. For the rain cell, add an extra label to the left of the picture. Change the font family of every label to **American Typewriter** with a font size of `16` and the rain label to `14`. Set the first picture to `sun` and the second one to `rain`.

In both the layouts, the date label located at the center of the cell must have the number of lines set to two. Change it in their attribute inspector. The final layouts should be like the following screenshot:

Finish the layouts by adding constraints to them. For the first cell, add these constraints:

- Image leading the superview with 0
- Image width 43
- Image bottom equals 0 to the superview
- Image top space equals 0 to the superview
- Image trailing equals default to the date label (the first label from the left)
- Image alignment bottom equals 0 to the date label bottom
- Image alignment top equals 0 to the date label
- Date label trailing space equals 0 to the temperature label
- Date label alignment Y equals 0 to the temperature label
- Temperature label trailing 0 to the superview
- Temperature label width equals to 56
- Temperature label top space equals 0 to the superview

For the second cell layout, use the following constraints:

- Rain label leading space equals 0 to the superview.
- Rain label width equals 64.
- Rain label bottom space equals 0 to the superview.
- Rain label trailing space equals 0 to the image.
- Rain label aligned on top with the image.
- Rain label aligned on bottom with the image.
- Image width 44.
- Image trailing space 0 to the date label.

- Image aligned bottom to the date label.

- Image aligned top to the date label.

- Date label top space equals 0 to the superview.

- Date label trailing space equals 0 to the temperature label.

- Temperature label trailing space 0 to the superview.

- Temperature label width equals 47.

- Temperature label bottom space equals 0 to the super view.

- Temperature label top space equals 0 to the superview. These constraints are for the cells, don't forget to add some of the constraints to the rest of the UI components (table view and labels).

Connect the components with their respective properties. However, if you connect the components by using the assistant editor, you might see that you are not able to connect the rain cell components to its code, as they are in the parent class. The easiest way to do this task is by dragging the components' reference from the Connections inspector to the cell in the document outline. The following picture demonstrates how you can do it:

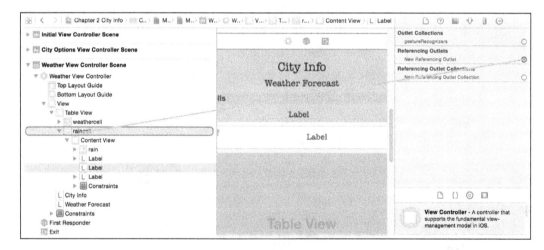

It looks like everything has been done, but is this scene going to be displayed? Of course not, we still need to add some code to instantiate this view controller and add it to the page view controller. Return to the `CityOptionsViewController` code and add the following highlighted code to its `viewDidLoad` method:

```
wikiViewController.cityInfo = self.cityInfo
cityViewControllers.append(wikiViewController)

let weatherViewController =
self.storyboard?.instantiateViewControllerWithIdentifier("weatherci
ty") as! WeatherViewController
weatherViewController.cityInfo = cityInfo
cityViewControllers.append(weatherViewController)

self.setViewControllers([wikiViewController], direction:
.Forward, animated: true) { (_) -> Void in
```

It is time to rerun the app and check whether there is a new page with a weather forecast similar to the following screenshot:

Retrieving some pictures

Now, we are going to display some pictures that were taken on the chosen city. As you know, we can use a table view for it. But, for this scenario, Apple has something more appropriate called the collection view.

Create a new file in the `ViewControllers` group called `PicturesViewController. swift`. Start by creating a class that inherits from `UICollectionViewController`:

```
import UIKit

class PicturesViewController: UICollectionViewController {
```

This class will need a special nested class to store the pictures' information, as we need to keep the URL, the title, the pictures ID, and the local path where it is stored:

```
private class PhotoInfo {
    var title:String!
    var url:String!
    var localPath:String!
    var id:String!
}
```

As properties, we just need the cityInfo and the array of PhotoInfo:

```
var cityInfo:CityInfo!
private var photos = [PhotoInfo]()
```

After this, we can initialize the array by requesting Flickr for a list of pictures and then we can download the pictures one by one. After each picture is downloaded, we are going to ask the collection view to reload its data. To do this task, we are going to use the following `viewDidLoad` method:

 This is not the best way to reload data, it could cause some lags if the broadband speed is very low. However, optimizing it would cause a huge code that would be hard to understand.

```
override func viewDidLoad() {
    let params:[String:String] = [
        "method": "flickr.photos.search",
        "api_key": "12345678901234567890123456789012",
        "text": cityInfo.name,
        "format": "json",
```

```
                      "extras": "url_t"
          ]



          requestJSON("https://api.flickr.com/services/rest",
          params: params) { (json, error) -> Void in
               for photo in json["photos"]["photo"].arrayValue {
                    if let url = photo["url_t"].string {
                         let photoInfo = PhotoInfo()
                         photoInfo.url = url
                         photoInfo.title = photo["title"].stringValue
                         photoInfo.id = photo["id"].stringValue
                         let documentDirectory =
NSSearchPathForDirectoriesInDomains(.DocumentDirectory,
.UserDomainMask, true)[0]
                         photoInfo.localPath = (documentDirectory as
NSString).stringByAppendingPathComponent("\(photoInfo.id).png")

                         self.photos.append(photoInfo)

                         if let url = NSURL(string: url){
                              NSURLSession.sharedSession().
downloadTaskWithURL(url){ (url,
response, error) in
                                   let urlTarget = NSURL(fileURLWithPath:
                                   photoInfo.localPath)
                                                      do {
                                        try
                                        NSFileManager.defaultManager().
moveItemAtURL(url!, toURL:
urlTarget)
                                   } catch _ {
                                   }
                                   M{
                                        self.collectionView?.reloadData()
                                   }
                                   }.resume()
                         }
                    }
               }
          }
     }
```

Table view data sources have a method called `numberOfItemsInSection`, so we also have it in collection views:

```
override func collectionView(collectionView: UICollectionView,
numberOfItemsInSection section: Int) -> Int {
    return photos.count
}
```

The other mandatory method for the data source is `cellForItemAtIndexPath`. Here, we are going to cause a compilation error as we don't yet have a class called `PictureCell`. Don't worry about it, we will fix it soon:

```
override func collectionView(collectionView: UICollectionView,
cellForItemAtIndexPath indexPath: NSIndexPath) ->
UICollectionViewCell {
    let cell =
collectionView.dequeueReusableCellWithReuseIdentifier("picturecell",
forIndexPath: indexPath) as! PictureCell

    if let data = NSData(contentsOfFile:
photos[indexPath.row].localPath) {
        cell.picture.image = UIImage(data: data)
    }
    cell.text.text = photos[indexPath.row].title

    return cell
    }
}
```

The `PicturesViewController` class is over. Now, add a new file called `PictureCell.swift` to the `Cells` group. Here, we will need only two properties: one for the picture and the other one for its title:

```
import UIKit

class PictureCell:UICollectionViewCell {
    @IBOutlet var picture: UIImageView!
    @IBOutlet var text: UILabel!
}
```

Go to your storyboard and add a collection view controller to it by dragging the collection view from the object library, as shown in the following screenshot:

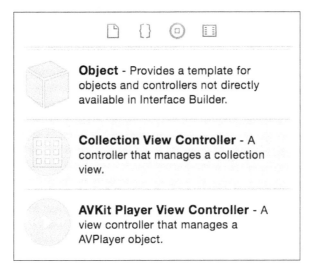

Select this new view controller and change its class to `PictureViewController` and its **Storyboard ID** to `picturescity`:

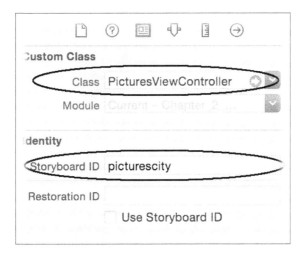

Now, click on the only cell we have in this collection view and change its class to `PictureCell`, identifier to `picturecell`, width to `128`, and height to `132`. Add an image view and a label to it. Set the number of lines of the label to 2. Connect the image and label with the corresponding properties in the `PictureCell` class and add constraints by clicking on the menu **Editor**, on the **Resolve Auto Layout Issues**, and then on add missing constraints.

Adding missing constraints is an option that helps us save time. However, you must take care. Frequently, the constraints are generated in the wrong way and you might need to redo some of them.

Now, to finish the app itself, we just need to instantiate `PicturesViewController` and add it as another page. Go to `CityOptionsViewController` and add the highlighted code to its `viewDidLoad` method:

```
cityViewControllers.append(weatherViewController)

let picturesViewController =
self.storyboard?.instantiateViewControllerWithIdentifier("pict
urescity") as! PicturesViewController
picturesViewController.cityInfo = cityInfo
cityViewControllers.append(picturesViewController)

self.setViewControllers([wikiViewController], direction:
.Forward, animated: true) { (_) -> Void in
    return
}
```

Rebuild the app and run it. Check whether you can see some pictures on the third page:

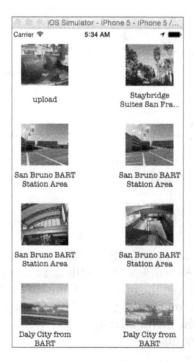

Summary

In this chapter, you learned how to create custom NSError, which is the traditional way of reporting that something went wrong. Every time a function returns NSError, you should try to solve the problem or report what has happened to the user.

We could also appreciate the new way of trapping errors with try and catch a few times. This is a new feature on Swift 2, but it doesn't mean that it will replace NSError. They will be used in different situations.

During the chapter, you learned the different ways of displaying options or a list of items on the screen. The table view is the most common one and we used it with custom cells. There is also the collection view controller, which works like a table view controller, but it can add cells horizontally and vertically. The other way is to use the page view controller, which is basically a table of view controllers.

The way we retrieved information was by using APIs. This is a very common way as internet connection is common these days. Of course, there are data that can't be stored locally due to storage space limitations (you can't have pictures of every city in the world on your phone) or because they need to be updated in a short period of time, like the weather.

In the next chapter, you are going to learn how to take a picture, edit it, and send it to your friends via social network.

3
Creating a Photo Sharing App

Nowadays, there is a big percentage of iPhone users who are also social network users. Don't ask how or why, you just have to accept this phenomenon. It implies that you probably may have to develop an app using social network APIs.

Another phenomenon that also comes with the popularity of smartphones is the camera usage. Basically, people have stopped buying traditional photo cameras and started using the camera that comes with their iPhones. There is a variety of reasons behind it and one of them is that they can take a picture with their phone camera and share it through their favorite social networking website.

Based on this fashion, in this chapter, we are going to develop an app to use the camera, edit pictures, and share them with our friends.

In this chapter, we will cover:

- Using the camera with `UIImgePickerController`
- Creating a custom `UIView`
- Manipulating an `UIImage`
- Posting on Facebook using Social Framework

Project overview

As we did in the previous chapter, let's start by getting a big picture of the application. We will then start coding.

Using this app should be very simple; remember that, nowadays, there are few users who read the manual. The user just needs to follow a few steps till he reaches the goal. Firstly, the user needs a photo, which can be taken from the camera roll or by using the camera. After this, the user can edit and add extra features to the picture. Once the user has finished treating the picture, he can share the picture with his friends.

Now that the app outline is done, we need to gather information on the features that are going to be used and whether they are viable or not.

The camera

There are different ways of using the camera, but what you really need to ask yourself is whether you need to use the camera's basic features or do you need to use some low-level features.

Low-level features might be used with the AVFoundation framework, which you are going to learn about in *Chapter 8, AVFoundation*. However, for this app, we don't need such features, so we can develop it faster using UIImagePickerController. This controller allows us to use the camera and the camera roll, and it also allows us to customize the layout.

Custom UIView

Custom UIView will allow us to modify the image chosen by the user and add some funny drawing before we share it with our friends on Facebook. To do this, we will have to store the elements added by the user. In the end, we can generate UIImage.

Such elements can be the background, a text, an image, and a shape. In this case, we are going to simplify it by creating texts with the same color and font family. There will only be one image (a hat) and the shape will always be a circle, but remember that you are free to improve this app.

The social framework

As social networks like Facebook and Twitter are very popular nowadays, Apple decided to create a framework for social networks, meaning that now it is much easier to share pictures with our friends.

For this app, we are going to use Facebook. The only detail the user must know is that he would have to log in to Facebook on his device before he uses this app.

 There are other ways of logging in to Facebook like using the SDK or some third-party frameworks such as Mixpanel. It depends on the users and the method they would like to use.

Logging in is not difficult; the user just needs to go to **Settings** and scroll down till they find the **Facebook** option.

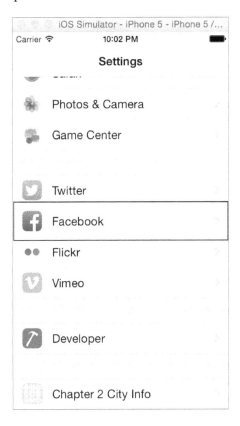

Once this option is selected, the user can introduce his username and password. He will then be able to post on Facebook using any iOS app.

Creating the app

Let's start creating the app by opening Xcode and creating a new, single-view application project. Call it Chapter 3 Photo Sharing and select **Swift** as its main language.

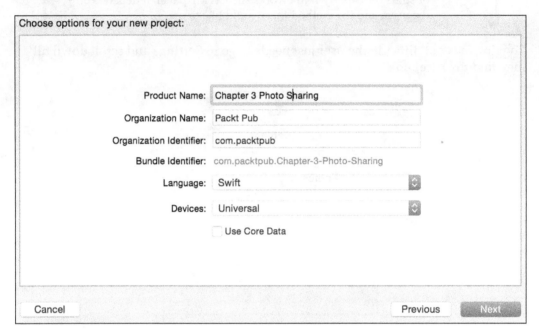

Before coding, we have to set the app configuration. In this case, we will set this app to be used only in the portrait mode. Click on your project, select the app target, and leave only the **Portrait** orientation checked.

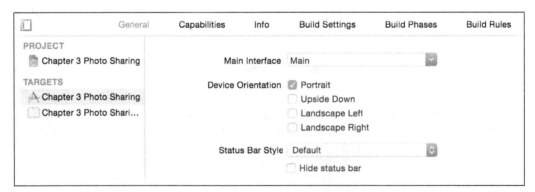

Rename the `ViewController.swift` file to `InitialViewController.swift` and do the same with its class. Don't forget to change the view controller's class on the storyboard.

Taking advantage of being on the storyboard, we can complete the layout of the first scene. This first scene just needs a title (a label), some user instructions (a text view), and two buttons: one to take a picture from the camera roll and another one to take a picture from the camera. Don't forget to add the `autolayout` constraints so it can be adapted to any screen size. The final layout will be similar to the following screenshot:

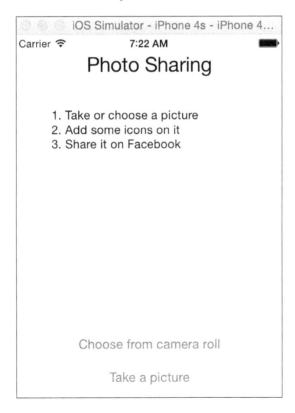

Even if your app should work only with the camera, it is a good idea to choose a picture from the photo gallery, even if it is a temporary option for development. This way, you will be able to test your app with the simulator.

For the instructions, let's make sure that the user is unable to change them. To do it, select the text view, go to its Attribute Inspector, and uncheck the **Editable** and **Selectable** options, as shown in the following screenshot:

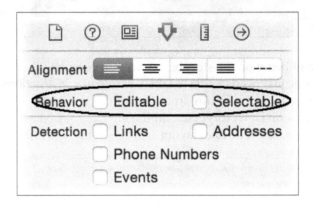

Connect each button to an action and call them `choosePhoto` and `takePhoto`. You can use the Assistant view to do it in a straightforward way. Leave these actions empty; we will complete them later:

```
@IBAction func choosePhoto(sender: UIButton) {
}
@IBAction func takePhoto(sender: UIButton) {
}
```

Now, we can complete this view controller. Let's start by completing the class definition. In this case, it needs to specify that the view controller is also an image picker controller delegate and a navigation controller delegate. Both delegates are required by `UIImagePickerController`:

```
import UIKit

class InitialViewController: UIViewController,
UIImagePickerControllerDelegate, UINavigationControllerDelegate {
```

As an attribute, the only one we will need is `UIImagePickerController`. This attribute will be in charge of taking a picture from the camera or from the photo gallery:

```
var imagePicker = UIImagePickerController()
```

We can then initialize this attribute by setting its delegate and do not allow any further modifications:

```
override func viewDidLoad() {
    super.viewDidLoad()
    imagePicker.delegate = self
    imagePicker.allowsEditing = false
}
```

Once we have the `imagePicker` setup, we can complete the button's actions. All we have to do is to set the attribute to where it should get the picture from and present it:

```
@IBAction func takePhoto(sender: UIButton) {
    // You can't switch these 2 lines order, otherwise your
    app will crash.
    imagePicker.sourceType = .Camera
    imagePicker.cameraDevice = .Front

    imagePicker.cameraCaptureMode = .Photo
    imagePicker.videoQuality = .TypeMedium

    self.presentViewController(imagePicker, animated: true,
    completion: nil)
}

@IBAction func choosePhoto(sender: UIButton) {
    imagePicker.sourceType = .PhotoLibrary
    self.presentViewController(imagePicker, animated: true,
    completion: nil)
}
```

Once the user takes the picture, the app will still need to know what to do with it. The `UIImagePickerDelegate` gives us two options: the first one is for when the user accepts the picture taken and the other one is for when the user cancels it. Both methods must be implemented, as we need to remove `imagePicker` from being displayed:

```
// MARK: - Delegate functions
func imagePickerController(picker: UIImagePickerController,
didFinishPickingMediaWithInfo info: [String : AnyObject]){
```

```
        imagePicker.dismissViewControllerAnimated(true,
        completion: { () -> Void in
            let image = info[UIImagePickerControllerOriginalImage]
            as! UIImage

            let editPictureViewController = self.storyboard?.
instantiateViewControllerWithIdentifier("editphoto") as!
EditPictureViewController
            editPictureViewController.photo = image
            self.presentViewController(editPictureViewController,
            animated: true, completion: nil)
        })
    }

    func imagePickerControllerDidCancel(picker:
    UIImagePickerController){
        imagePicker.dismissViewControllerAnimated(true,
        completion: nil)
    }
```

 If you allow photo editing, use the `UIImagePickerControllerEditedImage` constant instead of `UIImagePickerControllerOriginalImage` while retrieving the image.

Great! Now, we've got a compiler error. Don't worry about it for now; it is because we still need to implement another view controller. To finish this class, let's create the `unwind` method. This method will allow us to return to the first screen after we finish editing our photo:

```
    @IBAction func unwind(segue: UIStoryboardSegue){
    }
} // class end
```

Creating a view to draw on it

Before we start with the next view controller, we are going to create a custom view to draw the current picture's state and allow the user to add some features to it.

Create a new file called `BoardView.swift` and start a new class with the same name. This class must inherit from `UIView` (not `UIViewController`), therefore it needs to import `UIKit`:

```
    import UIKit

    class BoardView:UIView {
```

How is it going to work? It's very easy. We have to store the elements that should be drawn. Every time we store a new element, we will have to call `setNeedsDisplay` to report that there is something new. `drawRect` should be called as well. These elements are going to be implemented afterward; the only detail we need to know about them right now is that they inherit from a class that will be called `Element`, which will have a method called `draw`. Place the following code to add the elements to the array:

```
private var elements = [Element]()

func addElement(element:BoardView.Element){
    element.view = self
    elements.append(element)
    setNeedsDisplay()
}
```

After this, we will have to iterate over every element and draw it. As you can see, we just need to call a method called `draw`. It doesn't matter what kind of element it is.

```
override func drawRect(rect: CGRect) {
    for element in elements {
        element.draw()
    }

}
```

Now, we can create the last method for this class. It will collect the whole image with its icons and convert them into `UIImage`. This way, we can use our result to publish it on Facebook. This method creates a bitmap graphic context, which is like an image destination with the current `BoardView` frame size. It will wait till the board view is updated with the final image and convert the context into `UIImage` using the `UIGraphicsGetImageFromCurrentImageContext` function:

```
func getImage() -> UIImage {
    UIGraphicsBeginImageContext(self.frame.size)
    self.drawViewHierarchyInRect(self.frame,
    afterScreenUpdates: true)
    let image = UIGraphicsGetImageFromCurrentImageContext()
    UIGraphicsEndImageContext()
    return image

}
```

Is this class over? The answer is no! The Element class mentioned before should be used only with this view, so it is a good idea to create it as a nested class, as well as the classes that are going to inherit from it.

Swift still has some limitations with nested classes, mainly while using them with the interface builder. Please bear this in mind.

For this class, we will need to store its position on `BoardView`. Every time it changes, we will have to call `setNeedsDisplay`. We also need to store `BoardView` where this element belongs to. Finally, we have to create a method called `draw`. As Swift doesn't have abstract methods, it will raise an error in case it is called directly from the base class:

```
class Element{
    var position:CGPoint? {
        didSet{
            self.view?.setNeedsDisplay()
        }
    }

    var view:BoardView?

    func draw(){
        fatalError("The function \(__FUNCTION__) shouldn't be
called from the base class")
    }
}
```

Once we have the base class, we can implement its derived classes. We will start with the background, which is a class that stores an image and draws it on the coordinate origin:

```
class ElementBackground:BoardView.Element {
    var image:UIImage
    init(image:UIImage) {
        self.image = image
        super.init()
        self.position = CGPointZero
    }

    override func draw() {
        if let position = self.position {
            image.drawAtPoint(position)
        }
    }
}
```

A similar class is `ElementPicture`. It differs from the background by being drawn based on its center. So, the user will be able to drag it in a more intuitive way:

```
class ElementPicture:BoardView.Element {
    var image: UIImage
    init(image: UIImage){
        self.image = image
        super.init()
    }

    override func draw() {
        if let position = self.position {
            let newPosition =
            CGPointMake(position.x - image.size.width / 2,
            position.y - image.size.height / 2 )
            image.drawAtPoint(newPosition)
        }
    }
}
```

Another kind of element is the text. With this element, the user can write a message on his picture and place it wherever he wants:

```
class ElementText:BoardView.Element {
    var text:String
    var attributes:[String:AnyObject]
    init(text:String, attributes: [String:AnyObject]) {
        self.text = text
        self.attributes = attributes
        super.init()
    }

    override func draw() {
        if let position = self.position {
            text.drawAtPoint(position, withAttributes:
            attributes)
        }
    }
}
```

The last type of element we are going to have is the circle. Note that now we have to override the position attribute as, the first time, it needs to store the initial position. It will then store the opposite corner of its frame. After this element, we can close both the classes (`ElementCircle` and `BoardView`):

```
class ElementCircle:BoardView.Element {
    var initialPoint:CGPoint?
    override var position:CGPoint? {
        get {
            return super.position
        }
        set (value){
            if initialPoint == nil {
                initialPoint = value
            }
            super.position = value
        }
    }

    override func draw() {
        if let initialPosition = self.initialPoint,
        position = self.position {
            let borderRect =
            CGRectMake(initialPosition.x, initialPosition.y,
            position.x - initialPosition.x,
            position.y - initialPosition.y)
            let context = UIGraphicsGetCurrentContext()
            CGContextSetRGBStrokeColor(context, 1.0, 1.0, 1.0,
            1.0)
            CGContextSetRGBFillColor(context, 0.0, 1.0, 0.0,
            1.0)
            CGContextSetLineWidth(context, 2.0)
            CGContextFillEllipseInRect (context, borderRect)
            CGContextStrokeEllipseInRect(context, borderRect)
        }
    }
} // class end
} // class end
```

Developing the edition space

Return to the storyboard and add a new view controller to it. Here, we will have to perform a few steps. We will start by creating the exit point by control-dragging it from the view controller icon (yellow circle with a square in it) to the Exit icon (a square with an arrow). The idea behind this is to create an exit point that will allow us to return to the main screen:

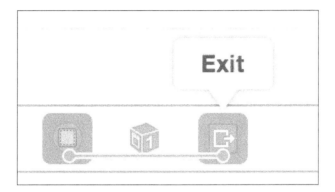

Once you release the mouse button, a popup will appear asking you to choose the exit point. In this case, there will be only one exit point called **Unwind**. Click on it and a new icon will appear on the document outline.

Select the symbol, go to its attribute inspector, and set its identifier to `restart`. Remember this identifier; we are going to use it later, while exiting to the main view.

We will now focus on the view controller's layout. We have to add three buttons to the top and set their titles to Text, Hat, and Circle, respectively.

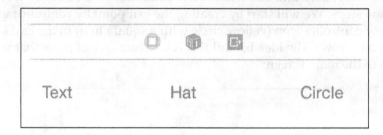

Under these buttons, add a new view. As everything has the word **View** on the object library, you can filter it by typing UIView.

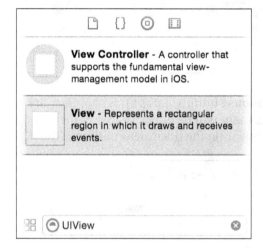

Select the view and, if you prefer, change its background color to gray, so it will be easier to visualize its size. Go to the identity inspector and change the class of UIView to BoardView.

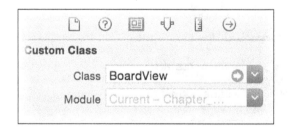

Resize the view by trying to occupy as much space as you can, but leave a gap at the bottom to add a new button. This button will be pressed by the user when he finishes editing his picture. Add the auto layout constraints you think are necessary. You can also add them with the magic of the suggested constraints. The main idea is to create a layout with three buttons at the top to represent the different types of elements that you can add to your image, a button at the bottom of the screen, and the board view to occupy the rest of the screen.

Now, we are going to implement the second view controller. Create a new file called `EditPictureViewController.swift`. Here, you have to import the `Social` framework besides `UIKit`:

```
import UIKit
import Social


class EditPictureViewController:UIViewController {
```

In this class, we will need three attributes: `boardView` will be connected to the one we have on the storyboard, `UIImage` is going to be the original photo received from the camera, and `BoardView.Element` (called `currentElement`) is the element we are working on at this moment. Every time the user releases his finger from the screen, we will consider that he has finished placing the current element. As a consequence of this, the attribute will be set to `nil`:

```
@IBOutlet var boardView: BoardView!
var currentElement:BoardView.Element?
var photo:UIImage!
```

Once the attributes are done, we can set up this view class with the `viewDidLoad` method. Here, we will need to add a gesture recognizer, as we need to track where the user is moving the current element:

```
override func viewDidLoad() {
    let element = BoardView.ElementBackground(image:
    UIImage(CGImage: photo.CGImage!, scale: 2, orientation:
    photo.imageOrientation))
    boardView.addElement(element)
    let gesture = UIPanGestureRecognizer(target: self, action:
    Selector("dragging:"))
    boardView.addGestureRecognizer(gesture)
}
```

As you saw in the previous code, we need to implement a method called `dragging` as the gesture handler. This method just needs to update the current element position. In case of releasing the finger from the screen, it needs to set that there is no current element anymore:

```
func dragging(gesture:UIPanGestureRecognizer){
    if let currentElement = self.currentElement {
        currentElement.position =
        gesture.locationInView(self.boardView)
        if gesture.state == .Ended {
            self.currentElement = nil
        }
    }
}
```

Now, we can create each button's action. Starting with the easiest, we are going to create the circle's action. It is as easy as creating the circle element and adding it to the board view:

```
@IBAction func addCircle(sender: UIButton) {
    currentElement = BoardView.ElementCircle()
    boardView.addElement(currentElement!)
}
```

Next, we can implement the hat. Here, the idea is very similar to the similar methods. The only difference is that we have to check whether the hat image was really loaded:

```
@IBAction func addHat(sender: UIButton) {
    if let image = UIImage(named: "hat") {
        currentElement = BoardView.ElementPicture(image:
        image)
        boardView.addElement(currentElement!)
    }
}
```

Remember that you have to copy the image from the book resources to `images.xcassets`, as shown in the following screenshot:

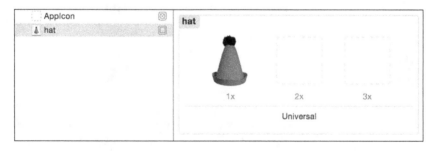

The third element, as you know, is the text. Here, the app must ask the user what text he wants to display. To do it, we are going to use an alert controller. Alert controllers are better designed than the previous alert view. Now, they are prepared to display text fields:

```
@IBAction func addText(sender: UIButton) {
    let alertController = UIAlertController(title: "Text",
    message: "Please introduce your text", preferredStyle:
    .Alert)
    alertController.addTextFieldWithConfigurationHandler {
    (textfield) -> Void in
        textfield.placeholder = "Write a message"
    }
```

Once we have set up the action—this is another difference against `UIAlertView`, as it doesn't use a selector anymore—it will use closures:

```
let action = UIAlertAction(title: "OK", style: .Default) {
(action) -> Void in
        let text = alertController.textFields!.first!.text!
        let textFontAttributes:[String:AnyObject] = [
            NSFontAttributeName: UIFont(name: "Helvetica",
            size: CGFloat(24.0))!,
            NSForegroundColorAttributeName:
            UIColor.redColor(),
            NSParagraphStyleAttributeName:
            NSMutableParagraphStyle.defaultParagraphStyle()
        ]

        self.currentElement = BoardView.ElementText(text:
        text, attributes: textFontAttributes)
        self.boardView.addElement(self.currentElement!)
    }
    alertController.addAction(action)
```

Note that, here, we used some predefined settings for the font. Right now, we have the Helvetica font with a font size of 24 and the color red, which is a style that is perfectly visible in most picture and screen sizes. Feel free to change them or add a feature where the user is able to change the current settings. An empty action is not mandatory, but it is good for the user. This way, he is able to cancel the text field in case he changes his idea:

```
let cancel = UIAlertAction(title: "Cancel", style:
.Cancel) { (_) -> Void in
    }
    alertController.addAction(cancel)
```

Now, you just need to present the alert controller by calling the presentViewController method:

```
        self.presentViewController(alertController, animated:
        true, completion: nil)
    }
} // class end
```

 Since the birth of iOS, there have been a lot of pop-up windows that are more attractive than the ones that are built-in. However, some of them have stopped being supported, which forced some developers to rewrite the corresponding code to keep the app up to date. Please think twice before you use any external popup.

Once the class is done, we have to update the storyboard. Return to the storyboard and select the view controller that we've been working on. Go to its Identity Inspector, update its class to EditPictureViewController, and set its **Storyboard ID** to editphoto, as shown in the following screenshot:

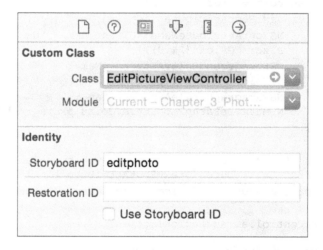

Before continuing with the rest of the code, it is a good time to test the app. Check whether you can take a picture and modify it by adding some circles, a hat, and some text messages. You might get a result similar to the following screenshot:

Publishing your picture

Now that you are able to edit the photo, we must develop the last part of the app. Connect the button at the bottom to an action called `done`:

```
@IBAction func done(sender: UIButton) {
```

Here, you have to check whether the user is able to post via Facebook. He may have not logged in. If he is able to post it, you can create a view controller for posting. You can then attach your picture to the view controller:

```
if
SLComposeViewController.isAvailableForServiceType(SLServiceTypeFacebook) {
        let fbViewController =
        SLComposeViewController(forServiceType:
        SLServiceTypeFacebook)
        fbViewController.addImage(boardView.getImage())
```

Now, we can set the operation that will be done when the user finishes with his post. In this case, if the user posts the picture correctly, we will return to first screen by using the `restart` segue:

```
        fbViewController.completionHandler =
        {(result) -> Void in
            switch result {
            case .Cancelled:
                ()
            case .Done:
                self.performSegueWithIdentifier("restart",
                sender: self)
            }
        }
```

Avoid "restacking" the view controllers; try using the unwind methods to return to the previous view controllers. It also frees the view controllers that were halfway in the process.

Present the view controller and close the if statement:

```
        presentViewController(fbViewController, animated:
        true, completion: nil)
    }
```

Now, we can complete this method by creating the `else` statement. It will tell the user that he needs to log in to post the picture:

```
else {
    let alertController = UIAlertController(title: "Log
    in", message: "You must log in on Facebook",
    preferredStyle: .Alert)
    let action = UIAlertAction(title: "Dismiss", style:
    .Cancel, handler: { (_) -> Void in
    })
    alertController.addAction(action)
    presentViewController(alertController, animated: true,
    completion: nil)
}
}// end done
```

It is time to test the app again. Run your app, take a picture, add some features (circles, texts, and hats), and try to publish it. Now, you should see a window that allows you to add a text and other options (**Location**, **Album**, and **Audience**) before you publish the photo:

Press **Post** and confirm whether your picture is published. How? It is very easy. Just open your web browser (on your computer or iPhone), log in to Facebook with the same account you have on your device, and check whether you have a new post on your wall.

 Avoid creating apps that submit many pictures, it can consume some broadband data and the user might be charged for it.

As you can see, the app works and you can have a lot of fun with your friends now.

Summary

In this chapter, you learned how to take pictures using the camera or the camera roll using `UIImagePickerController`. We were able to edit the taken picture using a custom view, which contains an array of elements. These elements were drawn using Core Graphics, which basically creates a context. Each call fills it with the corresponding function.

In the end, we were able to retrieve the edited picture and post it on Facebook, allowing us to share the final result with our friends.

In the next chapter, you are going to learn how to control your home devices using HomeKit.

4
Simulating Home Automation with HomeKit

For years, you might have been hearing about something called **Internet of Things (IoT)**, which is sometimes called **Internet of Everything (IoE)**. What is it all about? This new term applies to physical electronic devices that can be controlled by a computer or a mobile phone.

This concept isn't new. If you read about the origin of Java programming language, you will realize that it was done for home appliances. Things have changed and the market is now ready for this home evolution. Many companies have started investing in new products, therefore we will soon have doors, lights, TV, and refrigerators controlled by our mobile phones at our homes.

Apple has now released a new framework that allows developers to create apps that can control these devices.

In this chapter, we will cover:

- Installing the HomeKit Accessory Simulator
- Using the HomeKit framework

Project overview

This project consists of creating an app that will control the interiors of a living room and the garage door. In our living room, we have three accessories that can be linked to our iPhone or iPad: the door lock, fan, and aquarium thermometer.

When the app starts, it should set up the house if it is the first time, search for new accessories, and let the user choose the room that he would like to control or retrieve information from. If the user chooses the garage only, a view controller will be displayed, but if the living room is chosen as well, each accessory will be displayed in a different view controller that is controlled by UIPageViewController.

Preparing yourself for HomeKit

Let's get started with our HomeKit. The idea of this framework, as mentioned before, is to communicate the Apple device (iPhone or iPad) with a third-party device. The main question that arises when you use this framework is whether we need a physical device for developing with HomeKit. The answer is you don't need to buy any physical device; Apple provides us with a free simulator for development.

Of course, if you have a physical device, it would be worth testing on it. However, it is not essential. In the next section, you will learn how to download the HomeKit Accessory Simulator and see how to set it up.

Downloading the HomeKit Accessory Simulator

While developing with the HomeKit framework, start by downloading the HomeKit Accessory Simulator. This way, you won't need to buy any physical device. Open your Xcode. But, instead of starting a new project, click on the **Xcode** menu and then on **Open Developer Tool** and select **More Developer Tools...**.

There is another way of downloading the HomeKit Accessory Simulator, that is, when you enable the HomeKit capability on your project. Both ways take you to the same web page.

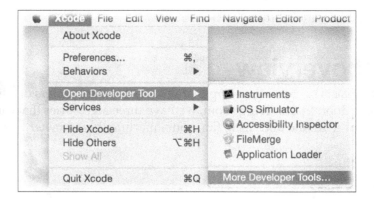

Your default web browser will open a download site in the Apple Developer Center. You might have to log in; if so, just do it and repeat the process. Once you have reached the download web page, look for Hardware IO Tools for your Xcode version and click on it to start downloading.

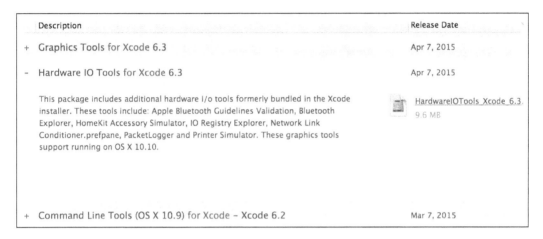

Once you have downloaded it, open the DMG file by double-clicking on it and drag the HomeKit Accessory Simulator to your `Applications` folder.

Creating accessories

Open the HomeKit Accessory Simulator by double-clicking on it (obviously). Now, you can add a new virtual accessory to your simulator. Start by clicking on the + sign located in the bottom-left corner of the window. Two options will appear: **New Accessory...** and **New Bridge...**; select the first one.

Let's create our first accessory. In this case, it will be a simple door lock that has only two states: locked and unlocked, which are going to be represented by a Boolean value. Complete the form that appears on the dialog box by writing `Door Lock` as the accessory's name and something like `Home Automation Limited` for the manufacturer.

A new accessory (`Door Lock`) will be listed on the left-hand side. Click on it and you will see a panel with the accessory's information with the following details:

- On the upper left-hand side, you can see the **Setup Code** ID. The user needs this code to link his app with the accessory.

- On the upper right-hand side, you can see a switch that turns your accessory's **IP** address on and off. Under this switch, there is a label that says **Pairings 0** with a **Reset** button next to it. While developing, you might need to click on the **Reset** button so you can lose your device's linkage.

- A button with the **Add Service** title can also be useful. However, for this first accessory, we won't use it.

- There is another button with the **Add Characteristic** title. We will have to click on it to add our door states.

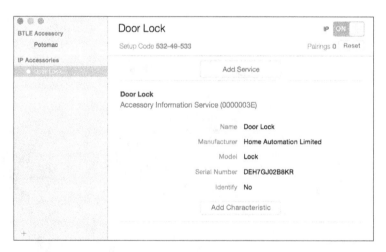

After clicking on the **Add Characteristic** button, a dialog will appear. In this case, you don't have to change anything, but copy the **UUID** value to eventually use it. Make sure that the format type is **Bool** and leave the rest of the fields empty.

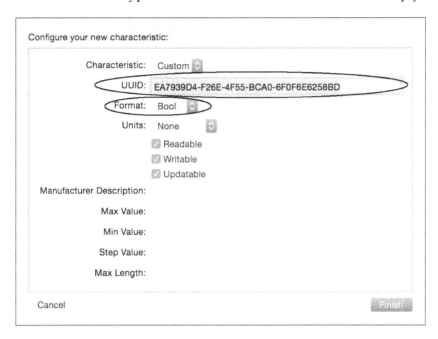

After pressing the **Finish** button, you will see that the characteristic has been created. You can change the initial value if you want.

Now that you know how to create new accessories, let's create some of them. Create a new accessory called `Fan`, which is supposed to be a fan in the living room. After creating it, instead of clicking on the **Add Characteristic** button, press the **Add Service** button.

Another dialog will appear but, this time, you will be able to choose a service type. Select **Fan Service**, press **Finish**, and take note of this accessory's setup code. Don't worry about the **UUID**; as it is a predefined service, we have constants to reach it.

Let's create the last accessory for our living room. We just need to receive some information from the aquarium temperature. Thus, we will create a new accessory called Aquarium Thermometer. Add a new service, select **Thermostat Service**, and press **Finish**. On the main panel, set the current temperature to 23.1 degree Celsius and the target temperature to 24 degree Celcius, as shown in the following screenshot. Take note of the setup code.

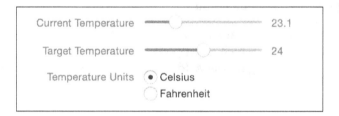

After this, we are going to create another accessory, but not for the living room. Now, we are going to create the garage door. Again, click on the **+** sign to add a new accessory and call it Garage Door. For this accessory, add a new service, that is, the Garage Door Opener Service and take note of the setup code.

Congratulations! You have a small virtual automated house. Now, you just need an app to control it.

Creating the app

Without closing the HomeKit Accessory Simulator, open Xcode and create a new project called `Chapter 4 Home Automation`. Check whether **Swift** is the main language and ensure **Use Core Data** is not checked.

Before we start coding, we will have to activate the ability to use HomeKit. Click on your project in the project navigator, select your project target (`Chapter 4 Home Automation`), click on the **Capabilities** tab, and turn **HomeKit** on.

Xcode will request you to select your enrolled Apple account for this feature. If you don't have one, it's about time you create it. HomeKit isn't the only feature that requests an enrolled Apple ID account.

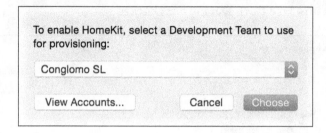

Now we are ready to start coding.

The first scene

The **first scene** must be in charge of setting up the house and then allowing the user to choose which room he wants to check. Our first task here is to rename the only view controller we have to something more expressive. Click on the `ViewController.swift` file and rename the file with its class to `SelectRoomViewController`. Don't forget to update the view controller name on the Attribute Inspector on the storyboard.

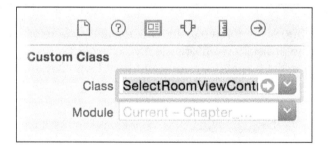

Continue by importing the HomeKit framework and setting this class as `HMHomeManagerDelegate`. This delegate will let us know when a home receives an update like when HomeKit loads information from homes, rooms, and so on:

```
import HomeKit

class SelectRoomViewController: UIViewController,
HMHomeManagerDelegate {
```

Now, we need to create an attribute of the `HMHomeManager` type. This way, we will be able to retrieve information on homes and in turn about the rooms and the accessories that are in them. Accessories are composed by services that have characteristics:

```
let homeManager = HMHomeManager()
```

Another attribute we will need is two buttons, each of them will take us to the corresponding room (the living room and garage). By default, they will be disabled till the information of their rooms is loaded:

```
@IBOutlet weak var livingRoomButton: UIButton!
@IBOutlet weak var garageButton: UIButton!
```

Once the attributes are defined, we need to initialize the home manager by setting its delegate. The manager will then start working and calling the delegates method if it is necessary. As we are on a view controller, this initialization should be done on the `viewDidLoad` method:

```
override func viewDidLoad() {
    super.viewDidLoad()
    homeManager.delegate = self
}
```

Before continuing with the `HomeKit` methods, we can create an unwind method, so we can return fast to this scene:

```
@IBAction func unwindMainMenu(sege: UIStoryboardSegue){
}
```

Now, we can create the `homeManagerDidUpdateHomes` method, which will be called at the beginning when the home manager loads the home information, even if there is no home set in the `HomeKit` database. Thus, we need to differentiate the case when there is no home—in which case, we will have to set it up—and when there is a home set—in which case, we will have to only enable the buttons:

```
func homeManagerDidUpdateHomes(manager: HMHomeManager) {
    if manager.homes.count == 0 {
        // There is no home set up, we must do it now.
        manager.addHomeWithName("Home Sweet Home",
        completionHandler: { home, error in
            if error != nil {
                // In case of error we will display it to the
                user
                self.displayError(error!)
```

```
                        return
                    }

            // as it is a new home we can set its rooms now
            home?.addRoomWithName("Living Room",
            completionHandler: {(room, error)-> Void in
                if error != nil {
                    self.displayError(error!)
                    return
                }
                self.livingRoomButton.enabled = true
            })
            home?.addRoomWithName("Garage", completionHandler:
            {room, error in
                if error != nil {
                    self.displayError(error!)
                    return
                }
                self.garageButton.enabled = true
            })
        })
    }else {
        livingRoomButton.enabled = true
        garageButton.enabled = true
    }
}
```

 This app is just a sample. This is the reason we are supposing that, if there is a home, it is the only one and its rooms should be already set. For real apps, it is better to check whether the home is the one that you want. If it is set, it is a good idea to check whether the rooms are also set.

Pay attention that the HomeKit methods usually are asynchronous. Remember, HomeKit communicates with the physical accessories via Bluetooth. It could take a long time for it to reply, technically speaking.

Let's create an auxiliary method that can search for a room using its name:

 Don't suppose that the rooms' array would always return them in the same order.

```
func getRoom(name:String) -> HMRoom? {
    if let home = homeManager.homes.first{
```

```
        for room in home.rooms {
            if room.name == name {
                return room
            }
        }
    }
    return nil
}
```

Now, we can prepare the `prepareForSegue` method. What does it mean? It means that we can't complete its code now, as we don't have the next view controllers. Thus, we should just leave a gap for them:

```
override func prepareForSegue(segue: UIStoryboardSegue,
sender: AnyObject?) {
    if sender === livingRoomButton {
        // TODO: Set the living room view controller
    }else if sender === garageButton {
        // TODO: Set the garage view controller
    }
}
```

This view controller is almost ready, except for one detail: it doesn't compile. The reason is that there is a method called `displayError`, which doesn't exists. So, let's create and make it available for every view controller by defining it as an `UIViewController` extension.

Create a new swift file (*command + N*) and call it `UIViewControllerExtension.swift`. Here, we just need to create the `displayError` method, which will show an alert controller with the error description:

```
import UIKit

extension UIViewController {
    func displayError(error:NSError){
        let alertController = UIAlertController(title: "Error",
        message: error.localizedDescription, preferredStyle:
        .Alert)
        let action = UIAlertAction(title: "Dismiss", style:
        .Cancel) { _ in
        }
        alertController.addAction(action)
        self.presentViewController(alertController, animated:
        true, completion: nil)
    }
}
```

Now, our code will compile it. As you can imagine, there isn't much to show. So, let's return to the storyboard and put two labels and two buttons on the only view controller we have till now. On the first label, write Home Automation to indicate the app's name and change its font size to **24**. For the second label, change its title to SELECT YOUR ROOM to give instructions to the user. Change the buttons' title to Living Room and Garage, respectively, and uncheck the **Enabled** checkbox on the attribute inspector of both the buttons.

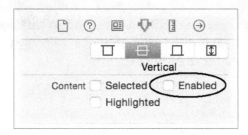

Connect the buttons to their corresponding attributes and place the components as in the following the screenshot. Don't forget to add some auto layout constraints.

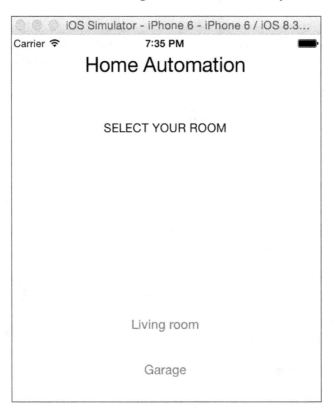

Now we can test our app. It will not do too much, but we will receive signs that the app is working fine. The first one is the HomeKit permission that must be asked when the app is launched. The second is the buttons state that would be changed to enabled, meaning that the home setup was done correctly. You might also receive an alert if you don't have the iCloud Keychain enabled.

Creating an accessory class

The first goal has been completed. Now, we can start developing the view controllers that represent the accessories with their states. As these view controllers need to be similar, we are going to create a common class.

Create a new file called `AccessoryViewController.swift`, click on it, and import `UIKit` and `HomeKit`:

```
import UIKit
import HomeKit
```

Let's create the `AccessoryViewController` class. It must inherit from `UIViewController` and it also needs to implement the `HMAccessoryBrowserDelegate` and `HMAccessoryDelegate` protocols. The first protocol is used to search for new accessories around us and the second one is used to detect instances when the current accessory changes its state:

```
class AccessoryViewController: UIViewController,
HMAccessoryBrowserDelegate, HMAccessoryDelegate {
```

As attributes, we will need `HMAccessoryBrowser`, the home object found on the first screen; the room object where the accessory belongs to; the accessory itself; the characteristics that we are controlling in the view controller; and one attribute that we are going to call: `acceptsNotifications`, which means that the accessory can notify the app when its state changes (like someone opened the door). It will also need three computed attributes that are the accessory names we are looking for, the service type, and the characteristic type. Why are these last two computed attributes needed? The reason is that they must be overridden:

```
var accessoryBrowser = HMAccessoryBrowser()
var home:HMHome!
var room:HMRoom!
var accessory:HMAccessory?
var characteristic:HMCharacteristic?
var acceptsNotifications = false
var expectedAccesory:String {
    get {
        fatalError("expectedAccesory should be called from an
        inherited class")
    }
}
var expectedService:String {
    get {
        fatalError("expectedService should be called from an
        inherited class")
    }
}
var expectedCharacteristic:String {
    get {
        fatalError("expectedCharacteristic should be called
        from an inherited class")
    }
}
```

As usual, after declaring the attributes, we are going to implement the `viewDidLoad` method. In this case, we need to check whether the accessory we are looking for is already assigned to its room. If so, we have to set its delegate and store it in the corresponding attribute:

```
override func viewDidLoad() {
    super.viewDidLoad()
    for accessory in room.accessories {
        if accessory.name == expectedAccesory {
            self.accessory = accessory
            self.accessory?.delegate = self
        }
    }
}
```

Now, we have to override the `viewDidAppear` method; in this case, we are going to do the opposite process of the `ViewDidLoad` method. If we don't have an accessory, we need to set the accessory browser and ask it to start looking for accessories. Otherwise, we can call a method that continues with the setup once the view controller knows that the accessory is found:

```
override func viewDidAppear(animated: Bool) {
    super.viewDidAppear(animated)
    if self.accessory == nil {
        accessoryBrowser.delegate = self
        accessoryBrowser.startSearchingForNewAccessories()
    }else {
        accessoryIsReady()
    }
}
```

Why did we do this part on `viewDidAppear` instead of doing it on `viewDidLoad`? The reason is very simple; we might instantiate and load a few view controllers at the same time. After they search for the accessories at the same time and each of them finds the corresponding accessory, we will assign them to their corresponding rooms. This action will request the user for the security code.

Now, imagine that your app extends to use 20 accessories and you are going to request their security code sequentially. It might be too exhausting to the user. You will have to write every accessory code when the first one appears on the screen. Wouldn't it be better if you wrote down the security while displaying it on the screen?

We order the accessory browser to search for new accessories. After this, we will have to implement the `delegate` method. Here, we will have to confirm that the accessory found belongs to the current view controller:

```
func accessoryBrowser(browser: HMAccessoryBrowser,
didFindNewAccessory accessory: HMAccessory) {
    print("Found: \(accessory.name)")
    if accessory.name == expectedAccesory {
        home.addAccessory(accessory, completionHandler: {
        error in
            if error != nil {
                self.displayError(error!)
                return
            }

            self.home.assignAccessory(accessory, toRoom:
            self.room, completionHandler: { error in
                if error != nil {
                    self.displayError(error!)
                    return
                }

                self.accessory = accessory
                self.accessory?.delegate = self
                self.accessoryIsReady()
            })
        })
    }
}
```

 Sometimes, it is also necessary to check the service name. Bear it in mind.

The method called `accessoryIsReady` is the one we just made up to act when the view controller is ready and to use the accessory with its characteristic. Bear this method in mind as it can be overridden when it is necessary. For this level of the class, it will search for its characteristic, set the notifications on if available, and read the current value:

```
func accessoryIsReady(){
    let accessory = self.accessory!
    for service in accessory.services {
        if service.serviceType != self.expectedService {
            continue
```

```
        }
        for characteristic in service.characteristics {
            if characteristic.characteristicType ==
            self.expectedCharacteristic {
                if let _ =
characteristic.properties.indexOf(HMCharacteristicPropertySupportsEven
tNotification){){
                    self.acceptsNotifications = true
                    characteristic.enableNotification(true,
                    completionHandler: { (error) -> Void in
                        if error != nil {
                            self.displayError(error!)
                            return
                        }
                    })
                }
                self.characteristic = characteristic
                self.readCharacteristicValue()
            }
        }
    }
}
```

We still need to complete the accessory delegate by reading the current characteristic value when a change is detected:

```
func accessory(accessory: HMAccessory, service: HMService,
didUpdateValueForCharacteristic characteristic:
HMCharacteristic) {
    self.readCharacteristicValue()
}
```

Now, we can finish this class by writing a method that should be overridden on the inherited class. This method should read the current characteristic value and update its representation on the screen. As it is quite characteristic-specific, we just need to define it and it will be overridden on the inherited class:

```
func readCharacteristicValue(){
    // this function should be overridden
}
} // end class
```

The basic class is done. Now, we are going to implement the garage view controller.

Building view controllers with HomeKit

Let's now get started with our controllers with the help of HomeKit. Basically, we will need a view controller for each accessory. In this app, the garage has only one accessory, therefore it has only one view controller. The living room has three accessories: the door, the fan, and the aquarium. As we have three accessories for the same room, we are going to use a page view controller to display the rest of the view controllers.

Bear in mind that the view controllers can be different. Information about a door that can be open or closed is not retrieved in the same manner as the aquarium temperature is received. However, every accessory has some common parts like the device name, the service, and the characteristic. This is the reason why each view controller must inherit from AccessoryViewController.

GarageDoorViewController

Now, we are going to implement our first visible accessory view controller. Here, we will need to use two images to represent the current garage door state. These pictures are called garageopen.png and garageclosed.png. They can be found in the book resources and you just need to drag them into the images.xcassets project.

Create a new file called GarageDoorViewController.swift and start coding it with a class that inherits from AccessoryViewController:

```
import UIKit
import HomeKit


class GarageDoorViewController:AccessoryViewController{
```

Starting with the attributes, we will need four of them: one is the value itself that will represent the last read door state (in this case, it is a Boolean value that represents whether the garage is closed); an UIImageView that will display the garage state to the user; and the two computed attributes that will help the class detect the desired accessory and characteristic:

```
var value = false
@IBOutlet var garageImage:UIImageView!
override var expectedAccesory:String {
        return "Garage Door"
}
override var expectedService:String {
```

```
        return HMServiceTypeGarageDoorOpener
    }
    override var expectedCharacteristic:String {
        return HMCharacteristicTypeTargetDoorState
    }
```

Every time we click on the garage door image, its state will change. As you can see, the garage door representation is an image not a button; it means that the tap event will be recognized by a gesture recognizer:

```
    @IBAction func toggleGarageDoor(sender:
    UITapGestureRecognizer) {
        let newValue = !self.value
        characteristic?.writeValue(newValue, completionHandler: {
        error in
            if error != nil {
                self.displayError(error!)
                return
            }
            self.readCharacteristicValue()
        })
    }
```

The next method is `readCharacteristicValue`, which is responsible for reading the accessory characteristic value and for updating the screen image. This is the last method of this class:

```
override func readCharacteristicValue() {
        characteristic?.readValueWithCompletionHandler({ error in
            if error != nil {
                self.displayError(error!)
                return
            }
            self.value = self.characteristic?.value as! Bool
            switch self.value {
            case true:
                self.garageImage.image = UIImage(named:
                "garageclosed")
            case false:
                self.garageImage.image = UIImage(named:
                "garageopen")

            }
        })
    }
} // end class
```

Pay attention that there is an attribute for the value of the characteristic. However, this value won't be updated if your accessory doesn't accept notifications. This is the reason it is preferable to use the `readValueWithCompletionHandler` method.

Garage layout

Once the garage code is ready, we have to create the visual part of that. Go to your storyboard, add a new view controller to it, select this new view controller, and change its class on the Identity Inspector to **GarageDoorViewController**.

Add a label, an image view, and a button to the image view controller. Change the label's title to `Garage` and place it at the top of the screen. Under it, place the image view. Place the button at the bottom of the screen. Set the image view to `garageclosed` and change the button's title to `Main screen`. Add the corresponding constraints and the final result will be something similar to the following screenshot:

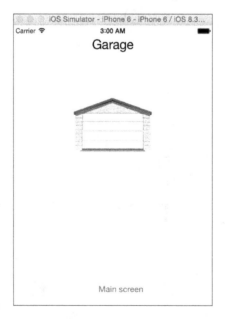

Connect the image view to its attribute and drag on it a tap gesture recognizer. This recognizer won't appear on the layout, but on the Document Inspector. Select the recognizer and open its Connections Inspector (*command + option + 6*). Drag the **selector** option from **Sent Actions** to the view controller icon and, once you release it, select the `toggleGarageDoor` method.

Now, we just need to create an action for our button. Control-drag it to the exit sign located at the top of the view controller. Select the `unwindMainMenu` method once you release the button.

For the last detail of this screen, you need to select the image view and check the **User Interaction Enabled** option on its Attribute Inspector (*command + option + 4*). Otherwise, when you touch on the garage door image, nothing will happen. Leveraging that you are here, change the image mode from **Scale to Fill** to **Aspect Fit**.

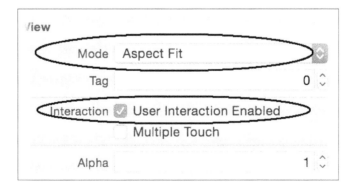

> We chose the **Aspect Fit** view mode, as we don't want to stretch the image like the **Scale to Fill** mode does. We didn't choose the **Aspect to Fill** mode, as it will increase the size of the image till there is no space left on UIImageView, cutting the part of the picture that is outside.

While the screen is ready, it will not appear as there is no mention of it on the main screen. On the same storyboard, click on the main screen view controller. Press control and drag the garage button to the garage door view controller to create the transition.

Go to the SelectRoomViewController.swift file; here, we still need to send some information to GarageDoorViewController. Scroll down to the prepareForSegue method and add the code for its corresponding part:

```
override func prepareForSegue(segue: UIStoryboardSegue,
sender: AnyObject?) {
    if sender === livingRoomButton {
        // TODO: Set the living room view controller
    }else if sender === garageButton {
        let accessoryViewController =
        segue.destinationViewController as!
        AccessoryViewController
        accessoryViewController.home = homeManager.homes.first!
        accessoryViewController.room = getRoom("Garage")
    }
}
```

This goal is done. Now, it is time to test the app and check whether it is working fine. Build and run your app (*command + R*) and tap on the **Garage** button. Don't forget that your HomeKit Accessory Simulator must be open. The first time it will say that the assigning accessory has no certificate; click on add it anyway. The app will then request for the security code; copy the one given in the HomeKit Accessory Simulator, as seen in the following screenshot:

Click on the garage door image and check whether the door opens and closes. Simultaneously, you will have to check whether, on the HomeKit Accessory Simulator, the target door state characteristic also changes (only target door state, don't worry about the other characteristics like current door state). This test means that your app is perfectly paired with the accessory and your actions (tapping on the door image) are also sending the right information.

Now, you have to test the app the opposite way by changing the target door state and checking whether the app image changes. This test means that the accessory is able to send notifications and is doing it correctly.

Building the living room

Once you are done with the garage door view controller, the process is straightforward for the rest of the accessories. You just need to consider some details; for example, in this room, we have more accessories. Due to this, we are going to show the view controllers with a page view controller.

Create a new file called `LivingRoomViewController.swift` and start creating a class with the same name. This class must inherit from `UIPageViewController` and will implement the `UIPageViewControllerDataSource` protocol. This protocol is for controlling the view controllers that will be displayed (see *Chapter 2, Creating a City Information App with Customized Table Views*) and also for displaying a page control, orienting the user about the current position:

```
import UIKit
import HomeKit

class LivingRoomViewController: UIPageViewController,
UIPageViewControllerDataSource{
```

As attributes, we need the home and the room as we have to resend them to the child view controllers and an array of accessory view controllers:

```
var home:HMHome!
var room:HMRoom!
var accessoryViewControllers = [AccessoryViewController]()
```

Now, we can initialize this view controller. We have two parts: the first part that creates and initializes the child view controllers and the second one that consists of changing the page control as, by default, it will be shown with a black background and white bullets and we would like to exchange these colors:

```
override func viewDidLoad() {
    super.viewDidLoad()

    // View Controllers
    let doorLock =
self.storyboard?.instantiateViewControllerWithIdentifier("doorlockview
controller") as! DoorLockViewController
    doorLock.room = self.room
    doorLock.home = self.home
    self.accessoryViewControllers.append(doorLock)

    let fan =
self.storyboard?.instantiateViewControllerWithIdentifier("fanviewcontr
oller") as! FanViewController
    fan.room = self.room
    fan.home = self.home
    self.accessoryViewControllers.append(fan)

    let aquarium =
self.storyboard?.instantiateViewControllerWithIdentifier("aquariumview
controller") as! AquariumViewController
    aquarium.room = self.room
    aquarium.home = self.home
    self.accessoryViewControllers.append(aquarium)

    self.setViewControllers([doorLock], direction: .Forward,
    animated: false, completion: nil)
    self.dataSource = self

    // Page control
    let pageControl = UIPageControl.appearance()
    pageControl.pageIndicatorTintColor =
    UIColor.lightGrayColor()
    pageControl.currentPageIndicatorTintColor =
    UIColor.blackColor()
    pageControl.backgroundColor = UIColor.whiteColor()
}
```

Complete this class with the data source protocol methods. The first two methods are for displaying the previous and next pages; the other two are for the page control:

```
// MARK: - Data source methods

    func pageViewController(pageViewController:
    UIPageViewController, viewControllerBeforeViewController
    viewController: UIViewController) -> UIViewController?{
        if let index =
self.accessoryViewControllers.indexOf(viewController as!
AccessoryViewController) where index > 0  {
            return self.accessoryViewControllers[index - 1]
        }
        return nil
    }
    func pageViewController(pageViewController:
UIPageViewController, viewControllerAfterViewController
viewController: UIViewController) -> UIViewController?{
        if let index = self.accessoryViewControllers.indexOf(
viewController as! AccessoryViewController) where index <
self.accessoryViewControllers.count - 1 {
            return self.accessoryViewControllers[index + 1]
        }
        return nil
    }

    func
presentationCountForPageViewController(pageViewController:
UIPageViewController) -> Int {
        // how many bullets should be displayed
        return accessoryViewControllers.count
    }

    func
presentationIndexForPageViewController(pageViewController:
UIPageViewController) -> Int {
        // position we start
        return 0
    }
} // end class
```

This file is over; but as you can see, we still need to implement the other view controllers.

The door lock view controller

Now, it is time to develop the door lock view controller. The operation is similar to that of the garage door controller; the difference is that its characteristic is a custom one and it is inside the identity service.

[Don't abuse the identity service. Try to create a new service, mainly when you have too many characteristics.]

Create a new file called `DoorLockViewController.swift` and create a class with the same name that inherits from `AccessoryViewController`:

```
import UIKit
import HomeKit


class DoorLockViewController:AccessoryViewController{
```

As attributes, we need the same ones that we had with the garage door, but we will update their values when required. Don't forget that the characteristic type is the number that was given to us when we created it:

```
var value = false
@IBOutlet var doorImage:UIImageView!
override var expectedAccesory:String {
    return "Door Lock"
}
override var expectedService:String {
    return HMServiceTypeAccessoryInformation
}
override var expectedCharacteristic:String {
    return "EA7939D4-F26E-4F55-BCA0-6F0F6E6258BD"
}
```

The door should open and close the same way as the garage door. It means that we just need to tap on the picture to open or close it:

```
@IBAction func toggleDoorLock(sender: UITapGestureRecognizer)
{
    let newValue = !self.value
    characteristic?.writeValue(newValue, completionHandler: {
    (error) -> Void in
        if error != nil {
```

```
                self.displayError(error!)
                return
            }
            self.readCharacteristicValue()
        })
    }
```

The method to display the door is also similar to that of the garage door, except that it does so with different pictures. Don't forget that you have to copy these pictures from the book resources and place them into the images.xcassets project. After this method, you can close the class:

```
override func readCharacteristicValue() {
    characteristic?.readValueWithCompletionHandler({ (error)
    -> Void in
        if error != nil {
            self.displayError(error!)
            return
        }
        self.value = self.characteristic?.value as! Bool
        switch self.value {
        case true:
            self.doorImage.image = UIImage(named:
            "doorclosed")
        case false:
            self.doorImage.image = UIImage(named: "dooropen")

        }
    })
    }
} // end class
```

The door is done. We will come back later to this class when we return to the storyboard.

FanViewController

Once the door lock is ready, we can create a class that is similar but with a few differences like `FanViewController`. Here, the idea is to use `UISwitch` to turn on and off the fan. The user will see the fan rotating on the screen, and to do it, we will need some help from some core graphics functions. Start importing `UIKit` and `HomeKit` and inheriting from `AccessoryViewController`:

```
import UIKit
import HomeKit


class FanViewController:AccessoryViewController {
```

As attributes, besides the traditional ones, we will need a reference to `UISwitch`. This way, we can set it to the right state when the view controller appears:

```
var value = false
@IBOutlet var fanImage:UIImageView!
@IBOutlet var fanSwitch: UISwitch!
override var expectedAccesory:String {
    return "Fan"
}
override var expectedService:String {
    return HMServiceTypeFan
}
override var expectedCharacteristic:String {
    return HMCharacteristicTypePowerState
}
```

Now, we have to create the method that turns on and off the fan. This method will be called by `UISwitch`:

```
@IBAction func toggleFanSwitch(sender: UISwitch) {
    let newValue = sender.on
    characteristic?.writeValue(newValue, completionHandler: {
    error in
        if error != nil {
            self.displayError(error!)
            return
        }
        self.readCharacteristicValue()
    })
}
```

After this, we can override the `readCharacteristicValue` method. Here, the operation is similar to the previous view controllers, except that we have to update the switch state and start animating the fan if it is on:

```
override func readCharacteristicValue() {
    characteristic?.readValueWithCompletionHandler({ error in
        if error != nil {
            self.displayError(error!)
            return
        }
        self.value = self.characteristic?.value as! Bool
        self.fanSwitch.on = self.value
        if self.value {
            self.rotateFan()
        }
    })
}
```

Lastly, we have to create the method that animates the fan. We are not going to use core animation, as it should be a very simple animation (rotation only). We will use the core graphics for this:

```
private func rotateFan(){
    UIView.animateWithDuration(NSTimeInterval(0.2), delay:
    NSTimeInterval(0.0), options:
    UIViewAnimationOptions.CurveLinear, animations: {
        self.fanImage.transform =
        CGAffineTransformRotate(self.fanImage.transform,
        CGFloat(M_PI / 2))

    }, completion: { finished in
        if self.value {
            self.rotateFan()
        }
    })
}
} // end class
```

AquariumViewController

The last view is the `AquariumViewController` class. This class is simpler than the previous ones for one small reason: a thermometer is not supposed to change the temperature, only read it. Create a new file called `AquariumViewController.swift` and a class with the same name:

```
import UIKit
import HomeKit


class AquariumViewController:AccessoryViewController{
```

The value attribute now is double instead of a Boolean value. Instead of an image, we are going to print the temperature on a label. The computed attributes are created with their corresponding values:

```
var value:Double = 0.0
@IBOutlet var temperatureLabel: UILabel!
override var expectedAccesory:String {
    return "Aquarium Thermometer"
}
override var expectedService:String {
    return HMServiceTypeThermostat
}
override var expectedCharacteristic:String {
    return HMCharacteristicTypeCurrentTemperature
}
```

Now, we can complete this class by reading its value and printing it on the label:

```
override func readCharacteristicValue() {
    characteristic?.readValueWithCompletionHandler({ (error)
    -> Void in
        if error != nil {
            self.displayError(error!)
            return
        }
        self.value = self.characteristic?.value as! Double
        self.temperatureLabel.text = "\(self.value) °C"
    })
}
} // end class
```

The code is almost over. Now, we need to go to the storyboard and complete the views.

The final storyboard

Click on the main file and place `UIPageViewController` in it. Create a transition by control-dragging it from the living room button on the main screen to the new page view controller. Click on this new view controller and on the Identity Inspector to change its class to `LivingRoomViewController`.

Go to the Attribute Inspector and change the transition style to **Scroll**. It will remove the page animation while it changes to the next view.

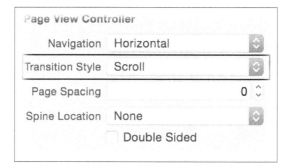

The page view controller is ready. Now, we need to create its view controllers. Drag a new view controller on the storyboard that will represent the door lock. Start by changing its class to `DoorLockViewController` and set its storyboard id to `doorlockviewcontroller`.

Create a layout similar to the garage door with a label, an image view, and a button on it. Add a tap gesture to the image and set its action to `toggleDoorLock`. Control-drag the button to the exit sign, change the label to **Door Lock**, connect the image view to its corresponding attribute, and set the image mode to `Aspect Fit`. The final result should be similar to the following screenshot:

Drag another view controller on the storyboard for the fan view controller. The operation is similar to the previous one. Start by going to the Identity inspector and changing its class to `FanViewController` and its storyboard id to `fanviewcontroller`. Add a label, an image view, and a button as we did for the previous view controller. But now, we have to add another component: `UISwitch`.

Here, you don't have to add the tap gesture recognizer as the switch will do an equivalent work for us. Change the label's title to `Fan` and the picture to `fan.png`, set the picture mode to `Aspect Fit`, connect the image view and the switch to their corresponding attributes, and drag the button to the exit sign. Another view controller is ready.

Now, we have to create the last view controller. Add a new view controller to the storyboard, change its class to `AquariumViewController`, and set its storyboard id to `aquariumviewcontroller`. Add two labels (one for the title and another for the temperature), an image view, and a button to it.

Change the button's title to **Main screen** and control-drag it to the exit sign. Set the image view picture to `aquarium.png` and change its mode to `Aspect fit`. Place the temperature label at the center of the picture; change its background color to blue, its text color to white, and its font size to 24; and connect it to the corresponding attribute.

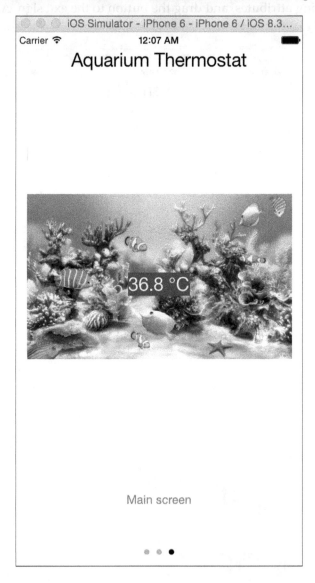

Great! Is everything done? The answer is no! We still need to update the code for the initial view controller to set living room in this house. So, click on the `SelectRoomViewController.swift` file, scroll down to the `prepareForSegue` method, and upgrade it with the highlighted code:

```swift
override func prepareForSegue(segue: UIStoryboardSegue,
sender: AnyObject?) {
    if sender === livingRoomButton {
        let accessoryViewController =
        segue.destinationViewController as!
        LivingRoomViewController
        accessoryViewController.home = homeManager.homes.first
        as! HMHome
        accessoryViewController.room = getRoom("Living Room")
    }else if sender === garageButton {
        let accessoryViewController =
        segue.destinationViewController as!
        AccessoryViewController
        accessoryViewController.home = homeManager.homes.first
        as! HMHome
        accessoryViewController.room = getRoom("Garage")
    }
}
```

Now, the app is ready and it is time to check it. Run the app and check whether it requests for the secure code the first time for each accessory. Also, check whether a change in their status changes the corresponding characteristic on the HomeKit Accessory Simulator and vice versa.

> While you are developing with HomeKit, you might need to reset the device's status. To do it, press the **Reset** button for every accessory. On the simulator, go to its menu and click on the **Reset Content and Settings...** options.

Summary

In this chapter, you learned how to use the HomeKit framework. This framework is supposed to be used with third-party physical devices, but Apple provides a simulator called the HomeKit Accessory Simulator.

We set some devices as well as created some services and received their security code. Once we had our virtual devices, we set a virtual home with virtual rooms and added home devices to them.

HomeKit works with asynchronous calls as they are done via Bluetooth. This is the reason why we had to switch threads while using the UI, check for errors, and also request for the current accessory value.

In the next chapter, you will learn how to control your health with HealthKit.

5
Health Analyzing App Using HealthKit

Wake up! Wake up! It's time to exercise! Otherwise, you are going to have a heart attack in a few days. This is the kind of phrase we are going to hear from our iPhones very soon, replacing a personal trainer with an app that knows everything about your health status at all times.

HealthKit is a new framework created to record your health status, which allows developers to create apps for fitness tracking or medical proposes. In this chapter, we are going to create an app that will use the HealthKit framework.

We will cover the following topics here:

- Requesting permission to use HealthKit
- Querying your health data
- Using an external framework to plot charts
- Reading and storing data with `NSUserDefaults`

Project overview

For this app, the idea is very simple; we just need to retrieve some information on the user such as the weight, the heart rate, and the number of steps. Then, we are going to display some graphs that will show the user's progress.

The setup

Let's start by creating a new app called `Chapter 5 HealthKit`. Make sure that **Swift** is the main language. We are not going to use Core Data, as HealthKit can store user data. We just need to know how to query this data. To store any information, we are going to use `NSUserDefaults`.

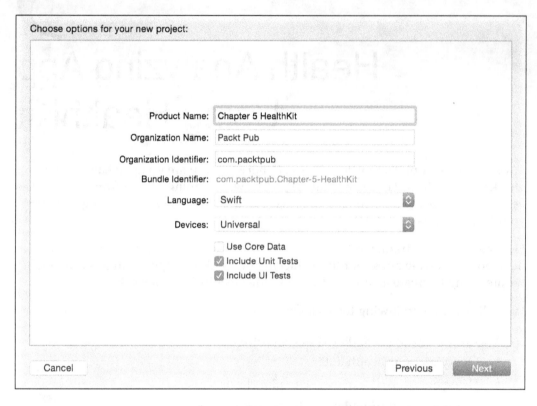

Click on your project in the project navigator, select the app target (`Chapter 5 HealthKit`), select the **Capabilities** tab, and turn on **HealthKit**. Xcode will ask you about your Apple account; this is a mandatory requirement to use this capability.

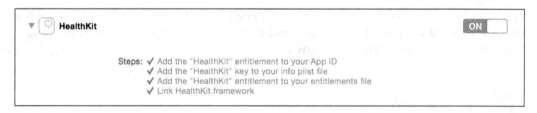

Before we start coding, we have to rename the only view controller to `InitialViewController`. Do it with the file name and the class name. After this, you will have to update the class name in the view controller attribute inspector.

Creating helpers

Before starting with the program, let's add some code that will help us through the app development process. Add a new file called `Helpers.swift` and add a helper function to execute the code in the main queue.

```
import Foundation

func M(block: dispatch_block_t){
    dispatch_async(dispatch_get_main_queue(), block)
}
```

 If you prefer, you can implement the M function in different ways. Some people prefer using `NSOperation` and some of them prefer using alternative frameworks like `Async` (`https://github.com/duemunk/Async`). It is up to you to choose the way it will be implemented.

Now create a new file called `Extensions.swift`. Here, we are going to add a function to display errors to the user, as we've already seen in the previous chapter. Place the following code in the new file:

```
import UIKit

extension UIViewController {
    func displayError(message:String){
        let alertController = UIAlertController(title: "Error",
        message: message, preferredStyle: .Alert)
        let alertAction = UIAlertAction(title: "Dismiss",
        style: .Cancel) { _ in
            self.dismissViewControllerAnimated(true,
            completion:nil)
        }
        alertController.addAction(alertAction)
        self.presentViewController(alertController,
        animated: true, completion: nil)
    }
}
```

Asking permission

The first view controller will contain three buttons that would be enabled only if the user allows the app to use HealthKit. So, start by clicking on the storyboard and adding a label and three buttons to it.

Place the label at the top and change its title to `Chapter 5 HealthKit`. Place two buttons at the center of the screen, disable all of them, and change their titles to **Your Current Data** and **Your Progress**. The final result is something similar to the following screenshot:

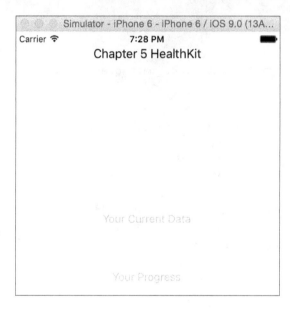

Drag two view controllers to the storyboard and connect each button to a different view controller. After this, link the buttons with the view controller as the outlet collection. An outlet collection is like an `IBOutlet`, but instead of connecting to a property of an object, you have to connect to an array property. This way you can iterate over every button, for example, and enable or disable them:

```
@IBOutlet var buttons: [UIButton]!
```

After this, we are going to create an enumeration for the weight units that are accepted by this app. This enumeration will be used to know the user's preference:

```
enum WeightType:String {
    case Kilogram = "Kilogram",
    Pounds = "Pounds",
    Stones = "Stones"
}
```

Return to the initial view controller and import the HealthKit framework:

```
import HealthKit
```

Now, we are going to override the `viewDidAppear` method, starting by initializing an object of the `HKHealthStore` type and the data that we would like to read and write from the user's health database:

```
override func viewDidAppear(animated: Bool) {
    super.viewDidAppear(animated)

    let healthKitStore:HKHealthStore = HKHealthStore()
    let weightQuantityType =
    HKQuantityType.quantityTypeForIdentifier(
        HKQuantityTypeIdentifierBodyMass)!
    let heartRateQuantityType =
    HKQuantityType.quantityTypeForIdentifier(
        HKQuantityTypeIdentifierHeartRate)!
    let stepCountType =
    HKQuantityType.quantityTypeForIdentifier(HKQuantityTypeIdentif
ierStepCount)!
```

After this, we have to check whether the device has the capability of using the HealthKit framework. Old devices and some earlier iOS versions are not compatible with HealthKit:

```
if !HKHealthStore.isHealthDataAvailable() {
    self.displayError("Health data is not available")
    return
}
```

Now, we have to create two sets, one for the features that we need to write (what is here called `ToShare`) and another for the features that we need to read:

```
let typesToShare = Set<HKSampleType>([weightQuantityType])
let typesToRead = Set<HKObjectType>([weightQuantityType,
    heartRateQuantityType, stepCountType])
```

Once you have instantiated the sets, you can request permission to use them. Note that, after receiving the reply from `requestAuthorizationToShareTypes`, we would have to execute the code in the main queue:

```
healthKitStore.requestAuthorizationToShareTypes(typesToShare,
readTypes: typesToRead) { success, error in
        M{
            if let error = error  {
                self.displayError(error.localizedDescription)
```

```
            }else if success {
                for button in self.buttons {
                    button.enabled = true
                }
            }
            else {
                self.displayError("Authorization not
                successful")
            }
        }
    }
} // end viewDidAppear
} // end class
```

The app is still in its initial stage, but it is time to test it. Build and run the app with *command* + *R*. When the app starts, you will see a screen asking the user for approval (see the following screenshot). After the user accepts it, the buttons will be enabled. This is the sign that everything is working fine.

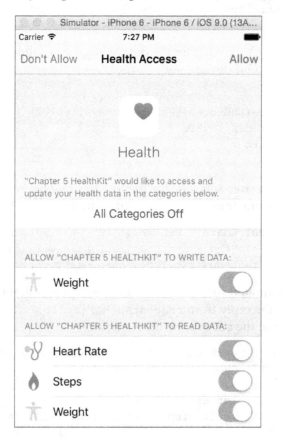

Displaying and saving the user's health data

Once we have done the main screen, we can start displaying the user data on a new scene. Here, we will display the number of steps and the heart beats in the labels and the weight and the weight goal in the text fields, as the user can change these values. We should also give the user the option of changing the unit for the weight (kilogram, pounds, and stones).

Create a new file called `CurrentDataViewController.swift`. Here, we will start by importing `UIKit` and `HealthKit`. After this, create a class with the name `CurrentDataViewController` that inherits from `UIViewController`:

```
import UIKit
import HealthKit

class CurrentDataViewController:UIViewController {
```

Now, we need to start with the attributes. Firstly, we need to create an attribute of the `WeightType` enumeration, which we created in `Helpers.swift`. This way, we could check the current user preference. Place the following code just after the class opening:

```
private var weightType:WeightType!
```

The next attributes are related to HealthKit; in this case, all of them are going to be declared and initialized together. The first property is an object of the `HKHealthStore` type. We used this object type on the first to request permission to use HealthKit, but here, we will use this object to retrieve the user's health data. The next three properties are the quantities of each data that will be retrieved, meaning that we will have to ask for an object of the `HKQuantityType` type using the predefined identifiers. Place the following code to declare these attributes:

```
private let weightQuantityType =
HKQuantityType.quantityTypeForIdentifier(HKQuantityTypeIdentifierBody
Mass)!
private let heartRateQuantityType =
HKQuantityType.quantityTypeForIdentifier(HKQuantityTypeIdentifierHear
tRate)!
private let stepCountType =
HKQuantityType.quantityTypeForIdentifier(HKQuantityTypeIdentifierStep
Count)!
```

Querying the user's health data requires a descriptor. This way, the health store will know the preferred order to return the data. In this case, we will always request for the newest one according to the end date, not the start date. Type the following code to declare the descriptor:

```
private let sortDescriptor = NSSortDescriptor(key:
HKSampleSortIdentifierEndDate, ascending: false)
```

The `HealthKit` framework stores the user data, but there is information that we need to store by ourselves, for example, the user's desired weight. This information must be stored at a different place and, for this app, we will use `NSUserDefaults` as we just need to save some data using the key-value pattern. Use the following code to create an attribute of the `NSUserDefaults` type:

```
private let userDefaults =
NSUserDefaults.standardUserDefaults()
```

The last attributes are the UI components. We will need two labels to display the heart rate and the number of steps and two text fields for the weight and the user's desired weight. Place the following code, but don't worry about connecting it to the storyboard:

```
@IBOutlet var stepCounterLabel: UILabel!
@IBOutlet weak var heartRateLabel: UILabel!
@IBOutlet weak var weightTextField: UITextField!
@IBOutlet weak var weightGoalTextField: UITextField!
```

It is time to initialize the attributes. Firstly, we need to read the preferred unit type for the weight, then we have to read the user data using auxiliary methods. Initialize the attributes with the following code:

```
override func viewDidLoad() {
    super.viewDidLoad()

    if let weightTypeString =
    userDefaults.valueForKey("weightType") as? String{
        self.weightType = WeightType(rawValue:
        weightTypeString)
    } else {
        userDefaults.setValue(WeightType.Kilogram.rawValue,
        forKey: "weightType")
        self.weightType = .Kilogram
    }

    // these functions read the current values, they will be
    implemented afterwards.
```

```
        self.readWeightGoal()
        self.readSteps()
        self.readHeartRate()
        self.readWeight()
    }
```

Let's fill these auxiliary methods in the same order that we called them. So, first, we will start with `readWeightGoal`. Here, we just need to read such data from the user defaults and update the corresponding text field. Put the following code in your class:

```
    private func readWeightGoal() {
        M{
            let unitLabel = UILabel()
            if self.weightType == .Kilogram {
                unitLabel.text = "Kg"
            }else if self.weightType == .Stones{
                unitLabel.text = "st."
            }else {
                unitLabel.text = "lb."
            }
            unitLabel.sizeToFit()
            unitLabel.textColor = UIColor.grayColor()
            self.weightGoalTextField.rightView = unitLabel
            self.weightGoalTextField.rightViewMode = .Always

            if let weightGoal =
            self.userDefaults.valueForKey("weightGoal") {
                self.weightGoalTextField.text = "\(weightGoal)"
            }
        }
    }
```

 The `rightView` as well as the `leftView` attributes were created for the purpose of completing the text view information like the unit type of a sample.

The next method is readSteps. Here, we have to create a query to give the desired result type, the number of samples (in this case, only one), and the result order (newest first). The query object also needs a handler to know what to do with the result. Once the query is created, the health store will have to call it, otherwise it will be just an object prepared to be called. Place the following code to read the steps:

```
private func readSteps(){
    let querySteps = HKSampleQuery(sampleType:
    self.stepCountType, predicate: nil, limit: 1,
    sortDescriptors: [sortDescriptor]) { query, results,
    error in
        if let error = error {
            self.displayError(error.localizedDescription)
            return
        }
        if let results = results where results.count > 0{
            let sample = results.first as! HKQuantitySample
            let steps:Int
            steps = Int(sample.quantity.doubleValueForUnit(HKUnit.
countUnit()))
            M {
                self.stepCounterLabel.text = "Number of steps:
                \(steps)"
            }
        }else{
            M {
                self.stepCounterLabel.text = "Number of steps:
                NO DATA"
            }
        }
    }
    healthKitStore.executeQuery(querySteps)
}
```

Ensure you always retrieve the quantity information given a specific unit. For the number of steps, it will always be countUnit. However, for other quantities like weight, you need to be specific with the measure you would like to use.

 In case of doubt, use the HKQuantity method isCompatibleWithUnit. This way, you won't ask for a nonsensical quantity.

Another detail that you have to be aware of is the UI updates that have to be done by sending them to the main queue; the reason is that the HealthKit query handlers are called on a different thread.

We can read the heart rate following the previous code. However, make sure you use the `countUnit` method in this code, but divide it by minutes as your unit should be beats per minute:

```
private func readHeartRate(){
    let queryHeartRate = HKSampleQuery(sampleType:
    self.heartRateQuantityType, predicate: nil, limit: 1,
    sortDescriptors: [sortDescriptor]) { (query, results,
    error) -> Void in
        if let error = error {
            self.displayError(error.localizedDescription)
            return
        }

        if let results = results where results.count > 0{
            let sample = results.first as! HKQuantitySample
            let bpm:Double
            bpm = sample.quantity.doubleValueForUnit(HKUnit.
countUnit().unitDividedByUnit(HKUnit.minuteUnit()))
                M {
                    self.heartRateLabel.text = "Heart Rate:
                    \(bpm)bpm"
                }
            }else{
                M {
                    self.heartRateLabel.text = "Heart Rate: NO
                    DATA"
                }
            }
        }
    healthKitStore.executeQuery(queryHeartRate)
}
```

Once we've understood the operation of querying, we can follow the same procedure for the weight. Here, we have to select the unit the user wants to display and convert it into a number. HealthKit works this way due to a logical reason: a quantity is a quantity and the unit you decided to use to store it will not matter. So, place this method to read the user's weight:

```
private func readWeight(){
    let queryWeight = HKSampleQuery(sampleType:
    self.weightQuantityType, predicate: nil, limit: 1,
    sortDescriptors: [sortDescriptor]) { query, results,
    error in
```

```
            if let error = error {
                self.displayError(error.localizedDescription)
                return
            }
            M{
                let unitLabel = UILabel()
                if self.weightType == .Kilogram {
                    unitLabel.text = "Kg"
                }else if self.weightType == .Stones{
                    unitLabel.text = "st."
                }else {
                    unitLabel.text = "lb."
                }
                unitLabel.sizeToFit()
                unitLabel.textColor = UIColor.grayColor()
                self.weightTextField.rightView = unitLabel
                self.weightTextField.rightViewMode = .Always
            }
            if let results = results where results.count > 0{
                let sample = results.first as! HKQuantitySample
                let weight:Double
                if self.weightType == .Stones {
                    weight = sample.quantity.
doubleValueForUnit(HKUnit.stoneUnit())
                }else if self.weightType == .Pounds {
                    weight = sample.quantity.
doubleValueForUnit(HKUnit.poundUnit())
                }else {
                    weight = sample.quantity.
doubleValueForUnit(HKUnit.gramUnitWithMetricPrefix(.Kilo))
                }
                M {
                    self.weightTextField.text = "\(weight)"
                }
            }else{
                print("No weight")
            }
        }
        healthKitStore.executeQuery(queryWeight)
    }
```

After coding the methods to read the user's data, we have to go the other way around: coding methods to write the user data. We will start by overwriting the user-desired weight, which should be done by setting a new value for the weightGoal key in NSUserDefaults.

```
private func saveWeightGoal(){
    if let weightGoal = Int(self.weightGoalTextField.text!) {
        userDefaults.setInteger(weightGoal,
        forKey: "weightGoal")
    }
}
```

In the next methods, we are going to write the user data using HealthKit. Bear in mind that we are not going to overwrite the current data, we are going to tell HealthKit to add new data. This way, we are able to see the progress. Use the following code to update the user's weight:

```
private func saveWeight(){
    let unit:HKUnit

    if self.weightType == .Kilogram{
        unit = HKUnit.gramUnitWithMetricPrefix(.Kilo)
    }else if self.weightType == .Stones {
        unit = HKUnit.stoneUnit()
    } else {
        unit = HKUnit.poundUnit()
    }

    if let value = Double(self.weightTextField.text!) {
        let weightQuantity = HKQuantity(unit: unit,
            doubleValue: value)
        let now = NSDate()
        let sample = HKQuantitySample(type:
        self.weightQuantityType, quantity: weightQuantity,
            startDate: now, endDate: now)
        healthKitStore.saveObject(sample, withCompletion: {
        (succeeded, error) in
            if let error = error{
                print("Failed to save the user's weight:
                \(error.localizedDescription)")
            }
        })
    }
}
```

The last methods we have to implement are the events that are going to be called by some buttons. Here, we have to know that there will be one button to change the weight unit and another one to save the data and return to the main screen.

Starting with the button that returns to the main screen, let's create an action that saves every piece of information and dismisses the view controller. Type the following code, but don't worry now about connecting it to the corresponding view:

```
@IBAction func saveAndClose(sender: UIButton) {
    self.saveWeightGoal()
    self.saveWeight()
    self.dismissViewControllerAnimated(true, completion: nil)
}
```

Now, let's create the event to change the weight. This event is going to show an action sheet with the units that are accepted by this app. After the user selection, it just needs to read the corresponding value again, convert it into the new unit, and place it in the corresponding view. As seen in the last method, we can also close the current class:

```
@IBAction func changeWeightUnit(sender: UIButton) {
    let alertController =
    UIAlertController(title: "Weight Unit",
    message: "Please choose your weight unit",
    preferredStyle: .ActionSheet)
    let setWeightType = { () in
        self.userDefaults.setValue(self.weightType.rawValue,
        forKey: "weightType")
        self.readWeight()
    }

    let kiloAction = UIAlertAction(title: "Kilograms",
    style: .Default) { _id in
        self.weightType = .Kilogram
        setWeightType()
    }
    alertController.addAction(kiloAction)

    let poundsAction = UIAlertAction(title: "Pounds",
    style: .Default) { _ in
        self.weightType = .Pounds
        setWeightType()
    }
```

```
        alertController.addAction(poundsAction)

        let stonesAction = UIAlertAction(title: "Stones",
        style: .Default) { _ in
            self.weightType = .Stones
            setWeightType()
        }
        alertController.addAction(stonesAction)

        presentViewController(alertController,
        animated: true, completion: nil)
    }
} // end CurrentDataViewController
```

Now, we can create the visible part of this scene. Click on the storyboard and go to the view controller that is connected to the user data button. Change its class in **Identity Inspector** to CurrentDataViewController. Drag five labels, two text fields, and two buttons to the layout, and change their titles to be as close as possible to the following screenshot:

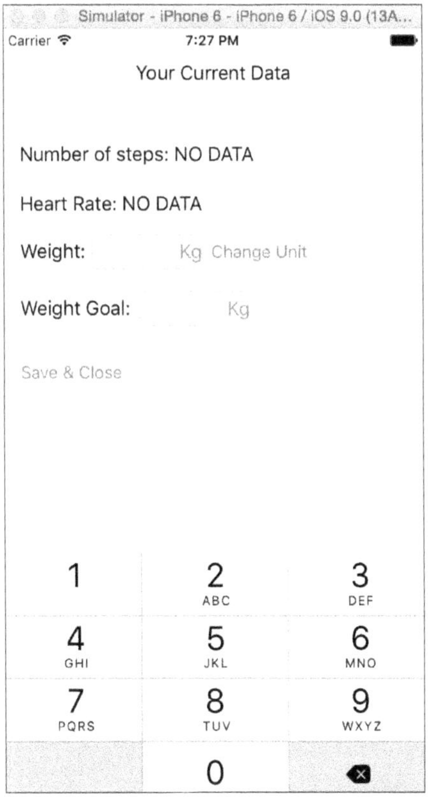

Link the buttons, the labels, and the text views to their corresponding attributes. Now, it is time to test the app again. Press Play and check whether you can save some data. After this, press the home key or *command + shift + H* on the simulator and go to the Health app, which is a built-in app with an icon of a heart:

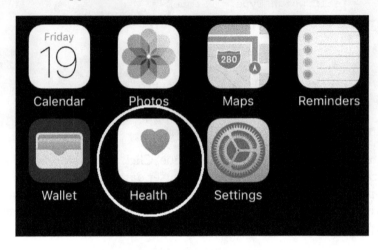

Check whether information you added is in its corresponding section. Do it the other way around as well; change some data here and check whether you can see your new data. Remember that weight goal is the only data that is not shown on the **Health** app, as it is stored using NSUserDefaults.

Checking your health record

The second button we have on the main screen is to display the user's history. As you can see, the Apple Health app displays some charts to show your data, but unfortunately, Apple doesn't provide these charts as UI built-in components. Thus, we have to use an external framework for it.

For this app, we are going to use a framework called iOS-Charts. To download this framework, open your favorite web browser and type the https://github.com/ danielgindi/ios-charts URL. Unzip the downloaded file and keep its path in mind.

Go to the general tab of your project's main target, scroll down to **Embedded Binaries**, and press the plus sign under it. A dialog will appear. In this dialog, click on the button with the **Add Other...** title. Here, you will have to choose the `Charts` projects from the previously unzipped file. Now, click on the plus sign of the next section (**Linked Frameworks and Libraries**) and choose **Charts.framework**. The result should be as follows:

Once **Charts.framework** is loaded, you have to build your project with *command + B* to check whether everything is compiled with your current Swift version.

 If you face syntax problems while compiling an external framework, try updating it to the latest Swift version (Edit, Convert, To the latest Swift Syntax). Swift changes very frequently.

Create a new file called `WeeklyChartsViewController.swift`, open it, and import `UIKit`, `HealthKit`, and the `Charts` framework, as shown in the following code:

```
import UIKit
import HealthKit
import Charts
```

Basically, what we want to do here is to create a view controller with three charts, one for the steps, another chart for the heart rate, and the last one to check the evolution of the weight. Each chart is an object of type `LineChartView` and should be declared as property. Thus, you need to open your class and place the chart's attributes as the following code:

```
class WeeklyChartsViewController: UIViewController{

    @IBOutlet var stepsChart: LineChartView!
    @IBOutlet var heartBeatChart: LineChartView!
    @IBOutlet var weightChart: LineChartView!
```

Continuing with the attributes, let's place the ones that come from HealthKit. We are already familiar with these attributes, as they are the same from the previous view controller. It means that we need a health store and three quantity types. Place the following code after the chart's attributes:

```
private let healthKitStore:HKHealthStore = HKHealthStore()
private let stepCountType =
HKQuantityType.quantityTypeForIdentifier(HKQuantityTypeIdentifierStep
Count)!
private let heartRateQuantityType =
HKQuantityType.quantityTypeForIdentifier(HKQuantityTypeIdentifierHear
tRate)!
private let weightQuantityType =
HKQuantityType.quantityTypeForIdentifier(HKQuantityTypeIdentifierBody
Mass)!
```

As we did for the previous view controller, we will need a sort descriptor to order the result. However, in this view controller, we are going to ask for the ascending order. We will also need a predicate for filtering, however, we are not going to initialize it here. So, we are going to leave it with an exclamation mark:

```
private let sortDescriptor = NSSortDescriptor(key:
HKSampleSortIdentifierEndDate,
    ascending: true)
private var predicate:NSPredicate!
```

The last attributes we need are the user's defaults to retrieve the user's preferred weight unit and weight goal, and another one to store the user's weight unit. Just place the following code in your class. We will then start with the methods:

```
private var userDefaults =
NSUserDefaults.standardUserDefaults()
private var weightType:WeightType!
```

Let's initialize this view controller with the `viewDidLoad` method. As you can see, most attributes are already initialized. We just need to initialize `weightType`, the predicate that filters data from one week and loads the chart's data:

```
override func viewDidLoad() {
    let currentDate =
    WeeklyChartsViewController.stripDate(NSDate())
    self.predicate = NSPredicate(format: "endDate >= %@",
currentDate.dateByAddingTimeInterval(-6 * 24 * 60 * 60))
    self.readSteps()
    self.readHeartRate()
    self.readWeight()
}
```

The next method that we are going to implement is the one for reading the user's steps, called `readSteps`, as you can see in `viewDidLoad`. Here, we are going to start by initializing a sample query, except that, in this case, we need to use our predicate for filtering and the limit should be 0, as there shouldn't be any limit:

```
private func readSteps(){
    let querySteps = HKSampleQuery(sampleType:
    self.stepCountType,
    predicate: predicate, limit: 0,
    sortDescriptors: [sortDescriptor]) {
    (query, results, error) -> Void in
```

Now, we need to check whether there is any error and display it if found:

```
if let error = error {
    self.displayError(error.localizedDescription)
    return
}
```

Great! Now, we have to sum every sample of each day. To do it, we are going to use a dictionary using a string that represents the month and the day as keys and a double as an accumulator. In this case, we are also going to use the keys as labels in our chart. This is the reason we have to use them as a well-formatted string:

 You don't need to use the dictionary keys as labels. It was done this way because this sample allowed us to. If it is necessary, instead of storing a double value, you can store an object with its value and label.

```
if let results = results where results.count > 0{
        var stepSum = [String:Double]()

        let dateFormatter = NSDateFormatter()
        dateFormatter.dateFormat = "MM/dd"
        for sample in results as! [HKQuantitySample]{
            let steps =
sample.quantity.doubleValueForUnit(HKUnit.countUnit())

            let dateString =
dateFormatter.stringFromDate(sample.endDate)
            if let _ = stepSum[dateString] {
                stepSum[dateString]! += steps
            }else {
                stepSum[dateString] = steps
            }
        }
```

After calculating, we can configure the chart view and feed it with some data. Firstly, we need to set some attributes to display messages and to disable user interaction:

```
        M{
            self.stepsChart.descriptionText = "Steps"
            self.stepsChart.noDataTextDescription =
"There is no step data"
            self.stepsChart.highlightEnabled = false
            self.stepsChart.dragEnabled = false
            self.stepsChart.setScaleEnabled(false)
            self.stepsChart.pinchZoomEnabled = false
            self.stepsChart.drawGridBackgroundEnabled =
false
```

The last part of this handler is to convert the data stored in the dictionary (`stepSum`) into chart entries. The values of the *x* axis must be stored as an array of strings, so we just need to retrieve the dictionary keys. The values of the *y* axis must be converted into an array of `ChartDataEntry` objects:

```
            let xVals = stepSum.keys.sort()
            var yVals = [ChartDataEntry]()
            for (i, key) in xVals.enumerate() {
                yVals.append(ChartDataEntry(value:
                stepSum[key]!, xIndex: i))
            }

            let dataset = LineChartDataSet(yVals: yVals,
            label: "Number of Steps")
            self.stepsChart.data = LineChartData(xVals:
            xVals, dataSets: [dataset])
        }
    }
}
```

Once the sample query is created, we just need to execute it and close the method:

```
        healthKitStore.executeQuery(querySteps)
    }
```

Now, we have to repeat the operation with the heart rate. The main difference is that here, you don't have to sum the heart beats, otherwise it would make no sense to do it. In this case, we have to display every sample, so we can see the rate variation:

```
    private func readHeartRate(){
        let queryHeartRate = HKSampleQuery(sampleType:
    self.heartRateQuantityType, predicate: predicate, limit: 0,
    sortDescriptors: [sortDescriptor]) { (query, results, error) ->
```

```
Void in
            if let error = error {
                self.displayError(error.localizedDescription)
                return
            }
            if let results = results where results.count > 0{
                var xVals = [String]()
                var yVals = [ChartDataEntry]()
                for sample in results as! [HKQuantitySample]{
                    let heartRate =
sample.quantity.doubleValueForUnit(HKUnit.countUnit().
unitDividedByUnit(HKUnit.minuteUnit()))
                    let dateFormatter = NSDateFormatter()
                    dateFormatter.dateFormat = "MM/dd"
                    let dateString =
dateFormatter.stringFromDate(sample.endDate)
                    xVals.append(dateString)
                    yVals.append(ChartDataEntry(value: heartRate,
                    xIndex: yVals.count))
                }
                M{
                    self.heartBeatChart.descriptionText =
                    "Heart Rate"
                    self.heartBeatChart.noDataTextDescription =
                    "There is no heart rate data"
                    self.heartBeatChart.highlightEnabled = false
                    self.heartBeatChart.dragEnabled = false
                    self.heartBeatChart.setScaleEnabled(false)
                    self.heartBeatChart.pinchZoomEnabled = false
                    self.heartBeatChart.drawGridBackgroundEnabled
                    = false

                    let dataset = LineChartDataSet(yVals: yVals,
                    label: "Heart Rate")

                    self.heartBeatChart.data =
                    LineChartData(xVals: xVals,
                    dataSets: [dataset])
                }
            }
        }
        healthKitStore.executeQuery(queryHeartRate)
    }
```

The last sample we have to read is the user weight. Remember that, to do it, the app must know the user's weight unit and goal. Create the following method to read the user's weight unit and the next one for the user's desired weight:

```
private func readWeightUnit(){
    if let weightTypeString =
    userDefaults.valueForKey("weightType") as? String{
        self.weightType = WeightType(rawValue:
        weightTypeString)
    } else {
        userDefaults.setValue(WeightType.Kilogram.rawValue,
        forKey: "weightType")
        self.weightType = .Kilogram
    }
}
private func readWeightGoal() -> Double?{
    return self.userDefaults.valueForKey("weightGoal") as?
    Double
}
```

The method to read the user's weight is called `readWeight`. Here, the idea is similar to the previous reading method, however, we have to consider some details. Even if it is not normal to change the weight more than once a day, we will consider the weight average of the day. For this reason, instead of storing only one number for each day as we did with the steps, we are going to store an array of numbers. Start this method with the following code:

```
private func readWeight(){
    self.readWeightUnit()
    let querySteps = HKSampleQuery(sampleType:
    self.weightQuantityType, predicate: predicate, limit: 0,
    sortDescriptors: [sortDescriptor]) { (query, results,
    error) -> Void in
        if let error = error {
            self.displayError(error.localizedDescription)
            return
        }
```

Now, we have to create a dictionary to store the weights set for each day and two optional variables to store the first weight of the week and the last one. This way we can check whether the user is approaching toward or moving away from his/her desired weight. The rest of the following code is similar to the equivalent one we have in the `readStep` method, except that here, we have to take care of the sample unit:

```
if let results = results where results.count > 0{
    var firstWeight:Double?
```

```
var lastWeight:Double?
var weightTable = [String:[Double] ]()
let dateFormatter = NSDateFormatter()
dateFormatter.dateFormat = "MM/dd"
for sample in results as! [HKQuantitySample]{
    let weight:Double
    switch self.weightType.rawValue {
    case WeightType.Stones.rawValue:
        weight =
sample.quantity.doubleValueForUnit(HKUnit.stoneUnit())
    case WeightType.Pounds.rawValue:
        weight =
sample.quantity.doubleValueForUnit(HKUnit.poundUnit())
    default:
        weight =
sample.quantity.doubleValueForUnit(HKUnit.gramUnitWithMetricPrefix(.
Kilo))
    }
    if firstWeight == nil {
        firstWeight = weight
    }
    lastWeight = weight



    let dateString =
    dateFormatter.stringFromDate(sample.endDate)
    if let _ = weightTable[dateString] {
        weightTable[dateString]!.append(weight)
    }else {
        weightTable[dateString] = [weight]
    }
}
```

Once we have filled the dictionary, we can initialize the weight chart. Remember that, for each day, we are going to show its average:

```
M{
    self.weightChart.descriptionText = "Weight"
    self.weightChart.noDataTextDescription =
    "There is no weight data"
    self.weightChart.highlightEnabled = false
    self.weightChart.dragEnabled = false
    self.weightChart.setScaleEnabled(false)
    self.weightChart.pinchZoomEnabled = false
```

```
                        self.weightChart.drawGridBackgroundEnabled =
                        false


                        let xVals = weightTable.keys.sort()
                        var yVals = [ChartDataEntry]()
                        for (i, key) in xVals.enumerate() {
                            let weightArray = weightTable[key]!
                            let weightSum = weightArray.reduce(0,
                            combine: { (sum, element) -> Double in
                                return sum + element
                            })


                            let avg = weightSum /
                            Double(weightArray.count)
                            yVals.append(ChartDataEntry(value: avg ,
                            xIndex: i))
                        }


                        let dataset = LineChartDataSet(yVals: yVals,
                        label: "Weight")


                        self.weightChart.data = LineChartData(xVals:
                        xVals, dataSets: [dataset])
```

This method is not over yet, now we have to report the user's progress with respect to his or her weight. If there is more than one sample, we have to check whether the user has reached his or her goal or whether he or she is approaching toward it or moving away:

```
    if results.count > 1 {
                        if let goal = self.readWeightGoal() {
                            let lastDiff = abs(goal - lastWeight!)
                            let firstDiff = abs(goal -
                            firstWeight!)
                            if lastDiff >= 0.0 && lastDiff <= 0.1
                            {
                                self.displayMessage("Congrats, you
                                have your desired weight")
                            }else if lastDiff < firstDiff {
                                self.displayMessage("You are doing
                                well")
                            }else {
                                self.displayMessage("Be carefull!
                                You are moving away from your
                                desired weight")
```

```
                          }
                    }else{
                        self.displayMessage("No desired weight
                        is set")
                    }
                }
              }
          }
      }
```

 Some iPhone models have the pedometer sensor to count the steps. The Apple Watch has a heartbeat sensor, however, there is no scale in any Apple device, so the weight will not be updated automatically.

The reason we had to compare `lastDiff` with a range is because doubles are not 100 percent accurate. Check `http://docs.oracle.com/cd/E19957-01/806-3568/ncg_goldberg.html` for more information.

Now, we can execute the query and finish this method:

```
        healthKitStore.executeQuery(querySteps)
    }
```

If you paid attention, you might have noticed that we called a method called `stripDate`. The idea of this method was to set till midnight the date given as an argument. This method is useful, as we would like to get NSDate from a week ago. So, we just need to set the current time to 0 and remove 6 days:

```
    private class func stripDate(date: NSDate) -> NSDate {
        let currentCalendar = NSCalendar.currentCalendar()
        let components =
    currentCalendar.components(NSCalendarUnit.Year.union(.Month).union(.
    Day), fromDate: date)
        return currentCalendar.dateFromComponents(components)!
    }
```

The last method of this class is a button event to close the current scene and return to the main menu. After this method, we can close the class:

```
    // MARK: UI methods
    @IBAction func close(sender: AnyObject) {
        self.dismissViewControllerAnimated(true, completion: nil)
    }
} // end WeeklyChartsViewController
```

Charts on the storyboard

Now, we can design the graphical part of this view controller. Click on the storyboard and go to the view controller that is connected to the button with the title Your Progress. Open its Identity Inspector (*command* + *option* + *3*) and change its class to `WeeklyChartsViewController`.

Drag three labels, three views and one button to the current view. Set the first label title to **Number of Steps**, the second one to **Heart Rates**, the third to **Weight**, and the button to **Close**. Under each label, place `UIView` and change their class to **LineChartView**:

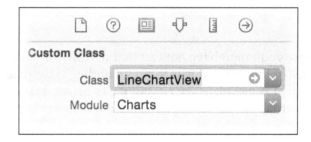

Connect the button to its corresponding method to close the scene and connect each `UIView` to its corresponding chart attribute. Move and resize them till you get a layout similar to the following screenshot. Don't forget to add the auto layout constraints.

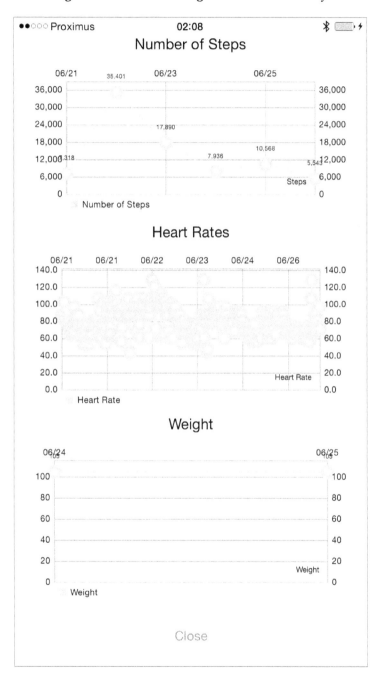

If you have any problem placing the charts on the storyboard, because they have the same color as the scene background, just temporarily change their background till you reach the desired layout.

Press Play and check whether the app is working. Try to use it for a week and check your progress.

Summary

Great! You have learned a new framework that gives information on the user's health. You can now query the phone, which requires you to convert the result into a quantity with a unit. It is done this way because a measure is a measure, it doesn't matter which unit is used.

You also learned, in this chapter, how to use the iOS-Charts framework, which allowed to display some charts of the user's progress, something very common in health apps.

In the next chapter, we are going to create our own game using the SpriteKit framework.

6

Creating a Game App Using SpriteKit

Since the creation of the first video game, 2D games are considered to be a big source of entertainment. There are big classic games like *Pac-Man* and *Super Mario Bros* that still entertain the new generation. As you know, smartphones and tablets can also be used as a new kind of video game console. There are games designed specifically for such devices that have become very popular like *Candy Crush*.

A developer can create a game using the traditional UI components like UIView and UIImage. However, its file size can get too heavy as these components are not specific to games. Due to this reason, Apple has created a framework especially for 2D game development called **SpriteKit**.

SpriteKit was created in a way that a developer needed only a few classes to use it, making it simple and useful.

In this chapter, we will cover the following topics:

- Creating scenes
- Creating nodes
- Different types of actions
- Checking for collisions
- Using the accelerometer sensor

Project overview

In this chapter, we are going to create a project called `Dino Surf`, which will give you an understanding of developing 2D games. The idea is very simple; the player will be a dinosaur that is practicing his favorite summer hobby: surfing. The user needs to turn the device to the right or to the left to dodge the birds and fishes that are moving on the screen. After a while, the enemies will arrive on the scene faster and faster.

The setup

Open your Xcode and create a new project. This time, instead of selecting **Single View Application**, you have to choose the **Game** template.

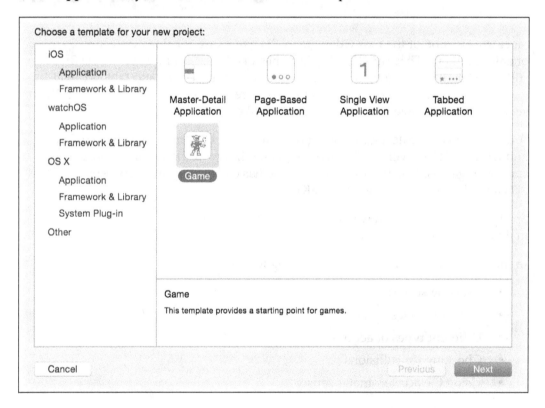

The preceding screenshot shows a template called **Game**. However, in the previous versions of Xcode, it was called SpriteKit. The name was changed due to the introduction of Metal and Scene Kit.

In the next dialog, some information will be required to set up the game. Set its name to `Chapter 6 DinoSurf` and ensure that **Swift** is its main language and **SpriteKit** is the chosen game technology. Your settings must be the same as it is in the following screenshot:

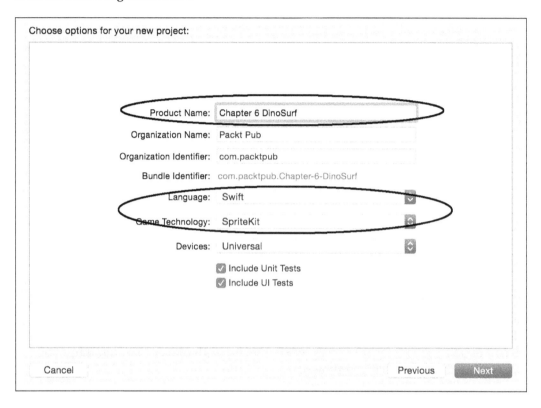

Then, choose the folder where you want to save the project and you will see your new project, however, you will appreciate a few differences. Instead of a file called `ViewController.swift`, you have `GameViewController.swift` and besides this file, you have two new files: `GameScene.swift` and `GameScene.sks`. Don't worry about the meaning or the content of each of these files; we are going to see it very soon.

Before we start coding, let's set the initial configuration. Select your project from the project navigator, click on the **General** tab, and change the deployment target to iOS 7.1. Leave only the **Landscape Right** orientation selected, as shown in the following screenshot:

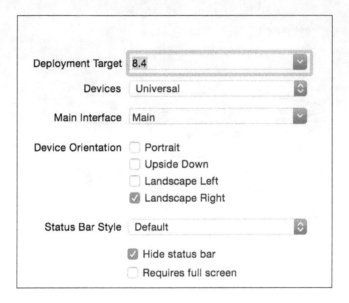

Click on the **Build Settings** tab and search for **Other Swift Flags**. Click on the left triangle to expand the **Setting** option and, in the **Debug** option, write -DDEBUG. The idea of this flag is to filter some code when the app is deployed. To sum it up, you just need to follow the scheme shown:

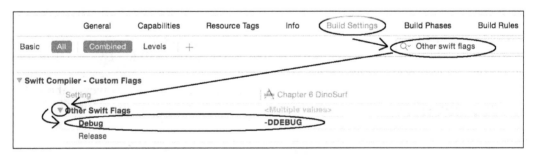

The flag we have added will allow us to filter some code using #if, #else, and #endif. Therefore, the final release product will be slightly different from the debugged one.

As games need very high performance, avoid leaving the code that is not necessary for the user, such as debug information, benchmarking code, and so on.

Let's complete the project setup by downloading the images provided by this book's resources and dragging them to the images.xcassets catalog, which is located in your project navigator inside the Chapter 6 DinoSurf group. Most of these images are PNG files, as we need transparency to have a cleaner visual effect.

 Developing games requires us to modify some images and retouch them. It is a good idea to learn some image manipulation programs such as Photoshop or Gimp.

Great! Now, we are going to press play to test the current app. You can use the simulator if you want to. However, later we will use the accelerometer sensor to move the dinosaur while turning the device. The accelerometer can't be tested with the simulator. You can rotate your simulator with the *command* + ← key combination.

The original game template simply displays the **Hello, World!** message at the center of the screen with information on the frames per second in the bottom-right corner. If you tap anywhere on the screen, a rotating spaceship will appear. Of course, this is not what we want, which is why we will have to remove some code soon.

Changing the current code

Now, let's start by changing the GameViewController class. Here, we don't have to make many changes. We just need to indicate whether the debug information will be displayed on debug compilations by using the preprocessor macro #if and #endif.

The scale mode will be changed to AspectFit. This way, we will be able to see the entire scene on the screen without it flowing over the screen borders. The default size of a SpriteKit project is 1024 x 768, which has an aspect ratio of 4:3. If you use a new device, the result will give you black bars on the sides. It is not an error; it is something that happens due to a different resolution ratio. Start wrapping the debug code between #if and #endif, as shown in the following highlighted code:

```
override func viewDidLoad() {
    super.viewDidLoad()

    if let scene = GameScene(fileNamed:"GameScene") {
        // Configure the view.
        let skView = self.view as! SKView
        #if DEBUG
            skView.showsFPS = true
            skView.showsNodeCount = true
            skView.showsDrawCount = true
        #endif

        skView.ignoresSiblingOrder = true

        /* Set the scale mode to scale to fit the window */
        scene.scaleMode = .AspectFit

        skView.presentScene(scene)
    }
}
```

It is not necessary to reinstall the app to test it; just recompile it with *command* + *B* to ensure that there is no syntax error. Now, go to the GameScene.swift file. Let's make some modifications, starting with an easy one. When the user taps on the screen, the app will pause or unpause. To do it, we just need to change the paused property by inverting its value. To summarize it, just replace the touchesBegan method with the following code:

```
override func touchesBegan(touches: Set<UITouch>, withEvent
event: UIEvent?) {
    self.paused = !self.paused
}
```

Easy, isn't it? Now it is time to initialize it; here, we will have to do it on the `didMoveToView` method. Replace the default one with a similar code that, instead of showing `Hello, World!`, shows `DinoSurf` using a blue font of the `Chalkboard SE` family:

```
override func didMoveToView(view: SKView) {
    /* Setup your scene here */
    let appTitle = SKLabelNode(fontNamed:"Chalkboard SE")
    appTitle.text = "DinoSurf";
    appTitle.fontColor = UIColor.blueColor()
    appTitle.fontSize = 65;
    appTitle.position = CGPoint(x:CGRectGetMidX(self.frame),
    y:CGRectGetHeight(self.frame) -
    CGRectGetHeight(appTitle.frame));
    self.addChild(appTitle)
}
```

Based on this code, we can create a similar code to display other kinds of information to the user. Now, we have to show: the current score that starts with 0, the number of lives that starts with 2, and the current level that starts with 1. Place this code at the end of the `didMoveToView` method:

```
let scoreText = SKLabelNode(fontNamed:"Chalkboard SE")
scoreText.text = "Score:";
scoreText.name = "label_score"
scoreText.fontColor = UIColor.blueColor()
scoreText.fontSize = 25;
scoreText.position = CGPoint(x: 0 ,
y:CGRectGetHeight(self.frame) -
CGRectGetHeight(scoreText.frame));
self.addChild(scoreText)

let levelText = SKLabelNode(fontNamed:"Chalkboard SE")
levelText.text = "Level:";
levelText.name = "label_level"
levelText.fontColor = UIColor.blueColor()
levelText.fontSize = 25;
levelText.position = CGPoint(x: 0 ,
y:CGRectGetMinY(scoreText.frame) -
CGRectGetHeight(levelText.frame));
self.addChild(levelText)

let livesText = SKLabelNode(fontNamed:"Chalkboard SE")
livesText.text = "Lives:";
livesText.name = "label_lives"
```

```
livesText.fontColor = UIColor.blueColor()
livesText.fontSize = 25;
livesText.position = CGPoint(x: 0 ,
y:CGRectGetMinY(levelText.frame) -
CGRectGetHeight(livesText.frame));
self.addChild(livesText)

self.refreshLabels()
```

We called a method called `refreshLabels`. This method will be called every time something has changed (the user score, the number of lives, or the current level). Till now, we don't have anything that controls these values, so we have to create them as properties outside `refreshLabels` (or if you prefer, at the beginning of the class). After this, we can develop the `refreshLabels` method:

```
var score = 0
var lives = 2
var level = 1

private func refreshLabels(){
    (self.childNodeWithName("label_score") as?
    SKLabelNode)?.text = "Score: \(score)"
    (self.childNodeWithName("label_level") as?
    SKLabelNode)?.text = "Level: \(level)"
    (self.childNodeWithName("label_lives") as?
    SKLabelNode)?.text = "Lives: \(lives)"
}
```

Build and run your app now to check whether the labels are appearing correctly. There will be no movement, as everything we put on the screen till now is static labels.

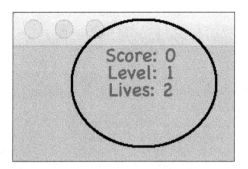

Adding a character and some waves

Now, it is time to add some life here. Let's put some water and the surfer dinosaur on the screen. To do it, we will need to create three `SKSpriteNode`: one for the character, another one for his wave, and a third one that will display some sea water. The first two nodes are going to be accessed by other methods; to do so, we are going to save them as an attribute. The third one (the sea water) will just be an animation that would be there forever, so we don't need to save it as an attribute or even give it a name. We will place these attributes on the top of the game scene class:

```
var wave:SKSpriteNode!
var dino:SKSpriteNode!
```

Go to the end of the `didMoveToView` method; here, we have to add some actions. An action is similar to an animation; in this case, we need to move the wave up and down, thus it will give a more realistic effect. As the up and down effect can't be done together, we will have to create another action that will be a sequence of actions. Lastly, we will have to create another action that will repeat the sequence forever, otherwise it will do it only once. Place this code at the end of `didMoveToView` to create the wave animation:

```
let waveUp = SKAction.moveByX(0, y: 20, duration: 0.5)
let waveDown = SKAction.moveByX(0, y: -20, duration: 0.5)
let waveUpAndDown = SKAction.sequence([waveUp, waveDown])
let waveMove = SKAction.repeatActionForever(waveUpAndDown)
```

There is no sense in creating animations and not applying them to anything. This is the reason we have to create a node to display the wave. We just need to instantiate the node, name it, set its animation, and place it as a view child. Theoretically, we also need to set its position, but we are going to do it later. So, we will place this code to create the game's wave:

```
wave = SKSpriteNode(imageNamed: "wave")
wave.name = "wave"
wave.runAction(waveMove)
self.addChild(wave)
```

What about the dinosaur? Basically we have to do the same operation, except that we have to use a different image and a different name.

```
dino = SKSpriteNode(imageNamed: "dinosaur")
dino.name = "dino"
dino.runAction(waveMove)
self.addChild(dino)
```

Once the wave and the character are added to the game scene, we have to place them at the right place on the screen. For now, we are just going to call a method that does it. The reason is that this method will be called when the player loses one life. Place this code after the dinosaur node creation.

```
self.startupPosition()
```

In order to compile our code, let's implement the startupPosition method. We just need to place the wave at the bottom of the screen and the dinosaur a little bit above it. Remember that, by default, the SKSpriteNode objects are instantiated with the anchorPoint attribute set to (0.5, 0.5), meaning that their positions are based on their centers. Place the following code at the end of the GameScene class:

```
private func startupPosition(){
    wave.position = CGPoint(x: CGRectGetMidX(self.frame), y:
    100)
    var dinoPosition = wave.position
    dinoPosition.y = wave.position.y + 3 *
    wave.frame.size.height / 4
    dino.position = dinoPosition
}
```

It's time to test the app again. So, we build and run it. Now, you can see that the app is alive; the dinosaur is above the wave and it is moving up and down like the arrow, as shown in the following screenshot:

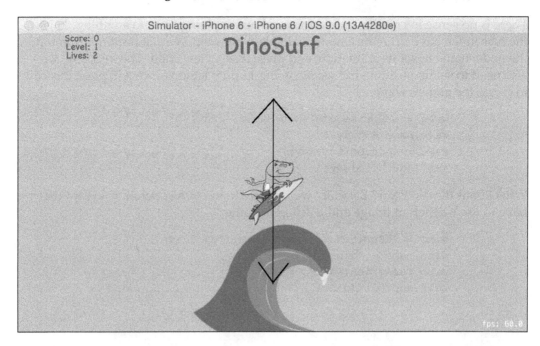

Don't forget that you can tap on the screen to pause and resume the game. To complete this stage, we can add the water picture at the bottom of the screen. The idea is very similar to one we had with the wave, except that in this case, instead of moving it up and down, the water will be moving forward and backward. This way, we will get an impression that the wave is not still.

Due to the reason mentioned previously, the actions will move on the *x* axis rather than the *y* axis. If you want, you can also change its duration. It will give an impression that the wave is either moving faster or slower. Return to the didMoveToView method and place the following code after the startupPosition call to add the sea and move it:

```
// water actions
let waterRight = SKAction.moveByX(10, y: 0, duration: 0.5)
let waterLeft = SKAction.moveByX(-10, y: 0, duration: 0.5)
let waterRightAndLeft = SKAction.sequence([waterRight,
waterLeft])
let waterMove =
SKAction.repeatActionForever(waterRightAndLeft)

// water node
let water = SKSpriteNode(imageNamed: "water")
water.position = CGPoint(x: CGRectGetMidX(self.frame), y:
0)
water.runAction(waterMove)
self.addChild(water)
```

Again, we have to rebuild and execute the app. Now, you will see that the sea water is moving forward and backward.

Creating some enemies

So far, we have only some animations on the screen. But, we need to add some enemies to make a more dangerous scenario.

In this game, we have two kinds of enemies — a dinosaur fish that jumps vertically from the water and a dinosaur bird, also known as a pterodactyl, which flies from the top of the screen to one of its sides.

When should we create an enemy? Actually, we can create them anytime; it is just a question of avoiding more than one enemy on the screen at the same time, otherwise the game would be very hard or almost impossible to play.

We could use NSTimer to schedule the enemies' appearance. Nonetheless, when we are talking about games, there is something that we have to consider. Usually, game engines and frameworks have a method that is called before rendering the frame, SpriteKit is no exception.

Note that the GameScene class has an overridden method called update. This method receives the current time as an argument, because according to the game, you have to calculate the difference of time between the current frame and the previous one. Although, we are not going to worry about it in this game, it is something we should consider.

> Don't assume that it will always be a fixed frame rate. It can vary during the game according to the device's workload. Some games have to lower the frame rate to get a better performance and to save battery.

Start checking whether there is any enemy on the screen by simply searching for any node named "enemy". If there is any node with this name, we will just ignore it. If there is no node named "enemy" we will call a function that will create it. Update the update method with the following code:

```
override func update(currentTime: CFTimeInterval) {
    if let _ = childNodeWithName("enemy") {}
    else {
        self.createEnemy()
    }
}
```

The `createEnemy` method has two options. The first one is to create a fish and the second one is to create a bird. It should be chosen randomly with the probability of each one being 50 percent. To do it, we are going to use `arc4random_uniform`, which returns a random number between zero and the argument minus one. To sum it up, the method in question is as simple as the following code:

```
private func createEnemy(){
    if arc4random_uniform(2) == 0 {
        self.createFish()
    }else {
        self.createBird()
    }
}
```

 If you would like more examples on random numbers in Swift, you can read *Swift Cookbook* by Packt Publishing.

Before we start implementing the `createBird` method, we have to analyze the bird's movement. It will start at any part of the top of the screen and move to one of its sides. If it starts at the left half of the screen, it will move to the right of the screen and vice versa. Its destination is a range from the top of the screen to its bottom, as shown in the following screenshot:

Based on the previous analysis, we can start creating the bird's node and setting its initial position. The horizontal position (*x* axis) is a random number based on the screen's width, and the vertical position (*y* axis) is always the top of the screen. Once you have understood this, you can place the following code in the GameScene class:

```
private func createBird(){
    let enemy = SKSpriteNode(imageNamed: "bird")
    let positionX =
    Int(arc4random_uniform(UInt32(CGRectGetWidth(self.frame))))
    enemy.position = CGPoint(x: positionX, y:
    Int(CGRectGetHeight(self.frame)))
    enemy.name = "enemy"
```

When the bird appears, it will first play a sound. To create this action, we are going to use the playSoundFileNamed method of SKAction. As the sound must be played parallel to the movement, you have to set the waitForCompletion argument to false:

```
let birdSound = SKAction.playSoundFileNamed("vulture.wav",
waitForCompletion: false)
```

Now, we will have to see the bird's destination. If the bird's start position is on the left-hand side of the screen, it must move to the right, and vice versa. The vertical position is based on the screen's height. It means that the bird can have its vertical destination at any point between the top and the bottom of the screen, so we are going to choose a random number based on the screen's height. After retrieving both the values, we can create the action to move the bird to its destination. Place the following code after the sound action is created:

```
    var destination = CGPoint()
    destination.y =
CGFloat(arc4random_uniform(UInt32(CGRectGetHeight(self.frame))))
    if CGFloat(positionX) < CGRectGetMidX(self.frame) {
        enemy.xScale = -1
        destination.x = CGRectGetWidth(self.frame)
    }else{
        destination.x = 0
    }
    let movement = SKAction.moveTo(destination, duration:
    self.duration)
```

Once the bird reaches its destination, we can remove it from the scene. Removing the bird from the scene will inform the `update` method that there is no enemy and it can create a new one. And then, we can create a sequence of actions that represents the full bird movement: playing the sound, moving the bird, and removing it from the screen:

```
let remove = SKAction.removeFromParent()
let sequence = SKAction.sequence([birdSound, movement,
remove])
```

The bird's actions are created and so is the bird node, but there is no relationship between the two. Now, we have to tell the node to execute the sequence of actions. When it finishes, the player will score one point.

The last step of this method is to add the node to the scene. The bird should then be able to do its job by itself:

```
enemy.runAction(sequence) {() in
    self.increaseScore()
}
self.addChild(enemy)
}
```

The method is ready, but there are some loose wires around it. Firstly, we are trying to load a file called `vulture.wav`, but this file is not yet in the project. Go to this chapter's resource folder, which was downloaded from the Internet, and drag the wave files (`vulture.wav`, `splash.wav`, `crunch.wav`, and `levelup.wav`) to your project. Make sure that the **Copy items if needed** option and the project target is checked, as shown in the following screenshot:

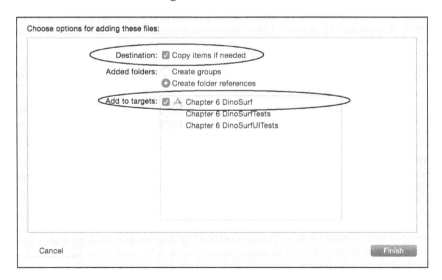

The next detail that wasn't declared is the `self.duration` attribute, which was used to set the period of the movements. The initial movement will last for 3 seconds, however, this time will decrease as the user climbs up the levels. Scroll up and place the following attribute:

```
var duration = 3.0
```

There is still another method called `increaseScore` that we have to implement. We will do it eventually after the `createFish` method is implemented.

Let's continue with the method that creates a dinosaur fish; the idea is similar to the previous method. The fish's initial position should be anywhere at the bottom of the screen. It means that the horizontal position (*x* axis) is a random number based on the scene width and the vertical position (*y* axis) is 0.

 Bear in mind that the origin coordinate (*x* and *y* equal to zero) on SpriteKit is in the bottom-left corner of the scene, not in the upper-left corner as in the UIKit.

Place the following code to start with the `createFish` method:

```
private func createFish() {
    let enemy = SKSpriteNode(imageNamed: "fish")
    let positionX =
Int(arc4random_uniform(UInt32(CGRectGetWidth(self.frame))))
    enemy.position = CGPoint(x: positionX, y: 0)
    enemy.name = "enemy"
```

Pay attention that this node is also called `enemy`. The reason is that, when the `update` method starts, it will look for any node with this name; it doesn't matter if it is a fish, a bird, or anything else. If there is one on the screen, it will simply ignore it; but if there is no node with the name `enemy`, it will create one.

Our fish image is in the horizontal position as if the fish was swimming. Nonetheless, we will have to rotate it 90 degrees to the left as it needs to be in the vertical position to jump/attack. To do it, we are going to change the `zRotation` property. After reaching the highest point, we are going to use an action called `rotateByAngle`. This action receives the degree of rotation in radians as an argument. Two pi radians are equivalent to 360 degrees; as we would like to rotate only 90 degrees, we need only half a pi radian. You can copy the pi value from the Internet; but it is not necessary, as Swift and Objective-C come with a constant for this number. So, we will add the following line to create the rotation action:

```
enemy.zRotation = CGFloat(M_PI / 2)
```

In this case, we could have rotated the image in the first place. We would have got a better performance, as the app wouldn't need to rotate it all the time. As this is not a complex game, the main goal is to teach SpriteKit. Here, it is done with the help of the code.

Now, we have to think about the fish attack. The whole animation should take the same time as the bird. But here, we have to divide it in three steps: prepare or wait, jump, and fall down. This is why we are going to start by calculating the duration of each step:

```
let stepDuration = self.duration / 3
```

The fish's first action is to just appear and wait a little while as if it is preparing to jump or just announcing its presence. For this kind of events, SpriteKit has the `waitForDuration` action:

```
let wait = SKAction.waitForDuration(stepDuration)
```

After waiting, the fish will jump. Translating this phrase to SpriteKit means that it will move from where it is to the center of the screen. This action is done together with the `splash.wav` sound:

```
let splashSound =
SKAction.playSoundFileNamed("splash.wav",
waitForCompletion: false)
let up = SKAction.moveToY(CGRectGetMidY(self.frame),
duration: stepDuration)
```

Once the fish has reached the highest point in the jump, it will fall down. First, we need to rotate 180 degrees, which is the same as pi radian. This will make the fish go upside down. Then, we have to tell it to return to its origin (y equals zero):

```
let fallRotation = SKAction.rotateByAngle(CGFloat(M_PI),
duration: 0)
let down = SKAction.moveToY(0, duration: stepDuration)
```

Once the fish falls back into the water, it must be removed from the scene. Now that we know the actions that are going to be performed by the fish and the sequence order, we can create an action that is the entire sequence:

```
let remove = SKAction.removeFromParent()
let sequence = SKAction.sequence([ wait, splashSound, up,
fallRotation, down, remove])
```

Great! The final part of this method is already known; we just need to run the actions and add the node to the scene. Remember that, if the node is able to finish its actions, it will imply that the player has successfully dodged it and scored one point:

```
enemy.runAction(sequence) {() -> Void in
    self.increaseScore()
}
self.addChild(enemy)
}
```

The final idea behind this fish jump is the movement shown in the following screenshot:

Now we can create the `increaseScore` method. Firstly, we just need to increase the score by one. So, we will place the following code to start with the method:

```
private func increaseScore(){
    self.score++
```

The second part of this method is to check whether the player has reached the next level. Here, we have to consider that, when we are testing, we need some sort of shortcuts. This will make our testing faster and help us detect issues sooner. The production game (the final compilation, the one that could be sent to the Apple App Store) will allow the user to go to the next level with every 10 points. It means that, when a user reaches 10 points, his level will be upgraded to 2; when he reaches 20 points, his level will be upgraded to 3. The development app (the one you have while developing) will upgrade the user's level every 3 points. So, we will place the following code to create the levelup constant:

```
#if DEBUG
    let levelup = 3
#else
    let levelup = 10
#endif
```

If the player has reached a new level, we can announce it by playing the levelup. wav file. This action will be released by the dinosaur. We don't have to worry much about who is playing the sound, as it doesn't create any visual effect. The duration attribute should also be reduced by 20%, making the enemies appear and leave faster. Thus, making the levels harder for the player:

```
if score % levelup == 0 {
    let levelup =
    SKAction.playSoundFileNamed("levelup.wav",
    waitForCompletion: false)
    self.dino.runAction(levelup)
    level++
    duration *= 0.8
}
```

We can finish this method by refreshing the labels; it will update the player's information:

```
        self.refreshLabels()
    }
```

Well done! You have reached the next stage of the app. Now you can build and run it. Here, you will see the bird flying, the fish jumping, and the scores and levels being updated. You are still not able to lose any life or move the character. These are our next goals.

Checking for collisions

Till now, the player doesn't lose his life on colliding with an object. When you tested the app at the end of the previous section, you saw the bird and the fish catching the dinosaur but nothing happened. The player scored a point even when the enemies touched the dinosaur.

Now it is time to fix it. Go to the `update` method and add the following highlighted code, which is just a call for a method called `checkOverlaps`, at the end:

```
override func update(currentTime: CFTimeInterval) {
    if let _ = childNodeWithName("enemy") {
        self.checkOverlaps()
    }
    else {
        self.createEnemy()
    }
}
```

The missing method is a simple one; here, we need to call a function named `enumerateChildNodesWithName`. This function will search for every node that has a name passed as the first argument, then execute the closure passed as the second argument. Leave the closure empty for now; just place the following code so you are still able to compile:

```
private func checkOverlaps(){
    self.enumerateChildNodesWithName("enemy") { enemy, stop in
    }
}
```

What should we do inside the closure? Here, we have to check whether the found enemy is overlapping with the dinosaur (only the dinosaur, not its wave). If so, we have to play the `crunch.wav` sound to let the user know that he or she has lost one life. We will have to remove the enemy from the scene, otherwise it will keep colliding with the dinosaur. We should call a method to decrease the player's life, but we will do it later. Place the highlighted code inside the enumeration handler:

```
self.enumerateChildNodesWithName("enemy") { enemy, stop in
    if enemy.intersectsNode(self.dino) {
        let crunch =
        SKAction.playSoundFileNamed("crunch.wav",
        waitForCompletion: false)
        self.dino.runAction(crunch)
        enemy.removeFromParent()
        // TODO: remove this comment self.decreaseLife()
    }
}
```

Time to test the app again. Press play and check whether, when an enemy touches the dinosaur, it makes a sound and disappears. Also, check whether the player scores a point.

Losing lives

Once the enemy reaches the dinosaur, we will have to decrease its life counter. If the life counter is greater than zero, we just need to decrease the life counter, call startupPosition to place the dinosaur at the center of the screen, and update the labels. This is the first part of the decreaseLife method:

```
private func decreaseLife() {
    if self.lives > 0 {
        self.lives--
        self.startupPosition()
        self.refreshLabels()
    }
```

What if it was the last life? In this case, we just need to remove the dinosaur from the scene and place a big label saying Game Over. Therefore, we can complete the decrease method with the following code:

```
    else {
        dino.removeFromParent()
        let gameOverLabel = SKLabelNode(fontNamed:"Chalkboard
        SE")
        gameOverLabel.position.x = CGRectGetMidX(self.frame)
        gameOverLabel.position.y = CGRectGetMidY(self.frame)
        gameOverLabel.fontSize = 65
        gameOverLabel.text = "Game Over"
        self.addChild(gameOverLabel)
    }
}
```

Great! Now, return to the checkOverlaps method, remove the following highlighted TODO comments, and check whether it is working or not:

```
// TODO: remove this comment self.decreaseLife()
```

Fixing the score counter

If you paid attention, you might have noticed something weird when the game ended; even if the dinosaur is not on the screen, the player will still score points. How could that be? It is possible because, every time the enemy reaches its destination, we call a method called `increaseScore`. This method just increases the score by one; the current state of the app doesn't matter.

We can solve it by first checking whether the dinosaur is on the screen before increasing the score. If the dinosaur is not on the screen, we can simply exit from the function. Fix the `increaseScore` function by adding the highlighted code:

```
private func increaseScore(){
    if self.children.indexOf(self.dino) == nil {
        return
    }
    self.score++
    ...
```

 In a more complex game, create an attribute that can be a Boolean value or an enumeration with the game state. This way, you will get a better performance than the one you will get by searching the array of nodes.

Is everything working as expected? The answer is, not yet. Note that the bird and the fish can still collapse with the nonexistent dinosaur. Again, the question is why?

The reason is that removing a node from the scene will not imply that it doesn't exist. The `intersectsNode` method simply checks the collision using their frames, not ensuring whether they belong to the same scene or not.

How can we solve this problem? The solution is similar to the previous one; we just need to go to the `checkOverlaps` function and check whether the dinosaur is on the screen. If so, we can enumerate the enemies node, otherwise the function won't do anything. Please update the `checkOverlaps` function with the highlighted code; don't forget to close its brackets:

```
private func checkOverlaps(){
    if let _ = self.children.indexOf(self.dino) {
        self.enumerateChildNodesWithName("enemy") { enemy,
        stop in
            if enemy.intersectsNode(self.dino) {
```

```
                    let crunch =
                    SKAction.playSoundFileNamed("crunch.wav",
                    waitForCompletion: false)
                    self.dino.runAction(crunch)
                    enemy.removeFromParent()
                    self.decreaseLife()
                }
            }
        }
    }
```

Build and run the app again. Now, if you wait a little while, you will not score and lose the game. The enemies will continue moving and won't disappear when they pass through the wave.

Moving the dinosaur

So far, more than playing the game, we watched it. The player was not able to interact with the game, except for pausing it. As it was told in the beginning of this chapter, the user is not supposed to touch the screen. He is supposed to play the game with the device in the landscape-right position and turn it to move the dinosaur as if it were a car wheel.

Now is the time when the accelerometer sensor will play a vital role. The accelerometer sensor allows us to know whether the user turned the device to the left or to the right. The principle of this sensor is a bit complex, but for this app, we just need to know that it will allow us to detect its orientation like a car wheel. You can read more about it at https://www.pc-control.co.uk/accelerometers.htm.

The old versions of iOS would work with a class called UIAccelerometer. But since iOS 4, we had to use a class called CMMotionManager. How do we use this class? First we have to import the CoreMotion framework. So, we will scroll up to the beginning of the GameScene.swift file and add the following line:

```
import CoreMotion
```

We will then declare an attribute called the manager of the CMMotionManager type:

```
var manager:CMMotionManager!
```

At the end of the didMoveToView method, we can instantiate this manager and call the startAccelerometerUpdates method with no arguments:

```
manager = CMMotionManager()
manager.startAccelerometerUpdates()
```

If you use `startAccelerometerUpdates` with a queue and a handler, it will create a pull of data received from the accelerometer, which might cause a delay in moving the character. For real time information, it is better to call `startAccelerometerUpdates` with no arguments.

The following picture shows how the axes are positioned on your device and where they have positive and negative values:

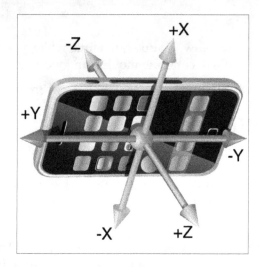

Now that you have understood these concepts, we just need to worry about the value of the *y* axis:

- **Positive value**: This means that the wave and the dinosaur should move to the left

- **Negative value**: This means that the wave and the dinosaur should move to the right

Moving to the left means that the position of the wave and the dinosaur will decrease. On moving to the right, it will increase. To think of it positively, we just need to multiply it by -1 when the dinosaur goes to the left, and multiply it by 1 when it goes to the right. So, let's create an enumeration inside this class to control these multipliers according to their sides:

```
private enum Direction: Int {
    case Left = -1,
        Right = 1
}
```

Now, we need to see the speed at which the wave is going to move. For this game, we are going to have three speeds:

- `Idle`: This means that the character should stay where it is
- `Slow`: This means that the character will move forward or backward by 5 points per frame
- `Fast`: This means that the character will move forward or backward by 10 points per frame

So, we will place the following enumeration after the `Direction` enumeration:

```
private enum Speed : Int{
    case Idle = 0,
    Slow = 5,
    Fast = 10
}
```

Great! Now, we are going to create a method that moves the wave and the dinosaur according to the requested speed and direction. Scroll down to the end of the `GameScene` class and start typing it in the following method header:

```
private func moveWave(direction:Direction, speed:Speed) {
```

The first thing we need to check is whether the speed is idle or the game is paused. In both cases, we won't move anything:

```
if speed == .Idle || self.paused {
    return
}
```

If the app reaches the next line, it will mean that the character and the wave will move. We can calculate the offset by retrieving the raw values of the direction and speed:

```
let offset = CGFloat(direction.rawValue * speed.rawValue)
```

Now, we have to check whether we are moving away from the screen. Technically speaking, the character can move beyond the screen limits. If we don't take care of it, we will have two problems:

1. The player might not know where the character is, as it is will not be visible anymore.
2. Someone might cheat by just moving the character away from the screen and scoring a lot of points.

For this reason, we have to check whether the movement is acceptable before we change the dinosaur's position. We can then close the method as everything is good to go:

```
if self.wave.position.x + offset > 0 &&
self.wave.position.x + offset < CGRectGetMaxX(self.frame)
{
    self.wave.position.x += offset
    self.dino.position.x += offset
}
}
```

Where should we call the method that was created? We should do it on the `update` method before the current code. Start by checking whether there is any accelerometer data. If so, create two variables, one for the speed with its default value as `Idle` and another one for the direction with the initial value as `Right`:

```
if let accelerationData = self.manager.accelerometerData {
    var speed = Speed.Idle
    var direction = Direction.Right
```

Now, we can set the speed by checking the force of the y axis. If its absolute value is greater than 0.5, we will consider it as high speed. If it is between 0.25 and 0.5, we will consider it as low speed. If it is lower than 0.25, it will stay idle:

```
if abs(accelerationData.acceleration.y) >= 0.5 {
    speed = .Fast
}else if abs(accelerationData.acceleration.y) >= 0.25
{
    speed = .Slow
}
```

Once we have the speed, we just need to check whether we have to switch directions as, by default, the character moves to the right. To do it, we just need to check whether the y axis returns a negative value. In this case, we have to set the direction to the left:

```
if accelerationData.acceleration.y > 0 {
    direction = .Left
}
```

Now, we can call the `moveWave` function and close the `if` statement:

```
self.moveWave(direction, speed: speed)
}
```

The final action

What should we do now? Press play and enjoy the game. Remember that you have to do it using a physical device, as the simulator can't simulate the accelerometer.

Check whether you can dodge the enemies and you can't move away from the screen. Once the game has your approval, you have to change its compilation to release it. To do it, click on the scheme pop up menu and go to the **Edit Scheme...** option:

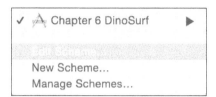

Ensure that you are on the **Info** tab of the **Run** section, click on **Build Configuration** and select **Release**, as shown in the following screenshot:

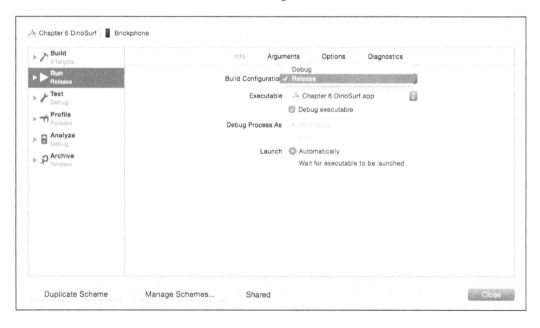

Press the **Close** button and run the game again. Check whether there is no debug information like the frames per second. To reach the next level, you have to score 10 points instead of 3. Have a lot of fun!

Summary

I hope you had a lot of fun with this chapter. You have learned how to use SpriteKit and have also enjoyed the game.

SpriteKit works in a very simple and logical way. You have to create nodes such as images and labels and animate them using actions. Actions can be moving, playing a sound, or rotating the node, or even a collection of actions like a group or a sequence.

You also learned how to use the accelerometer, making the game more enjoyable as you could move the dinosaur by turning the device like a car wheel.

In the next chapter, we will create an app for Apple Watches; hope you will enjoy it.

7
Creating an Apple Watch App

What time is it? It is time to go to the supermarket and get some supplies. It doesn't look like a traditional answer to this question. But believe me, watches will give you this type of an answer sooner or later. As we are now experiencing, mobile phones have multitude of functions other than making calls.

With the release of Apple Watch, we now have a new friend that tells us the time and advises us to stand up and walk away for a while because we've been seated for a long time. It demands attention, interrupts us constantly, and advises us on our food intake, ensuring that we do not gain weight. Basically, it is like a smaller version of a wife.

As it is a new product, many people are wondering about what this device can do and what are the forthcoming apps from this invention. Actually, there are some new apps in the process of being developed for this device. In this chapter, we are going to explore the development of a fridge control that would determine what is there in the fridge content and the duration of its lifetime. Furthermore, it will periodically advise you when your supplies are running low, so you can stock them up.

In this chapter, we will cover:

- Creating an Apple Watch extension
- Creating a glance
- Exchanging information between Apple Watch and the iOS app
- Testing the memory warnings
- Using the `MapKit` framework and retrieving directions

Project overview

The idea behind this project is to create an iOS app with an Apple Watch extension that will control the contents of your fridge. To set up the fridge contents, you need to use an iPhone device. However, the notification that the fridge is running out of food will be sent via Apple Watch.

You will also be able to use MapKit to guide you to the supermarket. The Watch app will only display the supermarket's location, while the iOS app will provide the directions to the supermarket.

 Till date, it has not been possible to create an Apple Watch app that is not linked to an iOS app, meaning that you always have to create an iOS app, even if it is an empty application.

watchOS 2 is the version you should use for this app; it is slightly different from the previous one. Ensure that you are using the correct simulator version or that you have updated your watch operating system. The Xcode version must be at least 7; don't use Xcode 6, except when you are developing for watchOS 1.

Setting it up

Open Xcode and click on **Create a new Xcode project**. This time, when the dialog appears, you have to click on the **Watch OS | Application** section and select the **iOS App with WatchKit App** option, as shown in the following screenshot. Once it is selected, press the **Next** button.

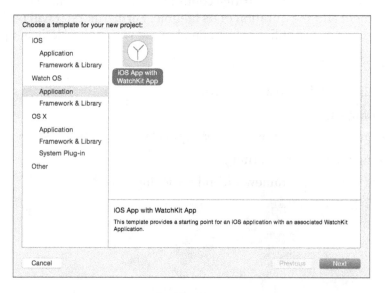

In the next dialog, set its title to `Chapter 7 Fridge Control` and make sure that the **Include Notification Scene**, **Include Glance Scene**, and **Include Complication** checkboxes are checked, as shown in the following screenshot. Curiously, the option to use Core Data is not available on this screen; however, you won't be needing it.

If you need to use Core Data for your project, there is a simple way to do it. Just create a single-view application with Core Data and add the WatchKit extension.

Although we would not be using complications, it would be a good idea to leave the app prepared for it.

Press **Next** and choose a folder for your project. When Xcode opens the project, you will see that the project has more files, groups, and schemes than it had before. While developing apps for Apple Watch, note that there will be two additional targets: the app extension that contains the code of your app and the app target that contains the storyboard and some resources.

 The first version of watchOS would install only the target app on the Watch and the extension was installed on the iPhone device. With watchOS 2, both the targets are installed on the watch. However, you still have two targets instead of only one.

Now, click on your project in the project navigation, select your project target, and go to the **Capabilities** tab. Search for the map's capability and turn it on. For this app, we are going to activate only the route by car. Once you know how it works, you can activate other routes later on.

This procedure must also be done on the Watch Extension target. This way, we can display the map on our watch.

Return to the iOS app target, click on the **Build Settings** tab, and scroll down to the **Swift Compiler** section. Expand the **Other Swift Flags** record and add the **-DDEBUG** debug option, as we did in the previous chapter. This way, we can have different settings when we are in development and when we are distributing the app.

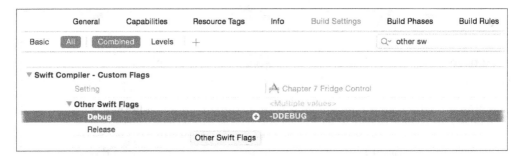

The iOS app

As it was mentioned before, this app will also be developed for iOS. The iOS app has two options:

- The first one is to add supplies to your fridge
- The second one is to check its current state

Inside the current state option, there will be another scene that will show us a map with the directions to the supermarket.

Rename the `ViewController.swift` file to `InitialViewController.swift`. Then, click on it and also rename its class to `InitialViewController`. Now, click on the storyboard and update the view controller class.

Drag one label and two buttons to the scene. Set the label title to `Fridge Control`, one button title to `Add supplies`, and the other one to `Check Status`. Don't forget to add the auto layout constraints that you think are necessary. The final result should be a simple layout similar to the following screenshot:

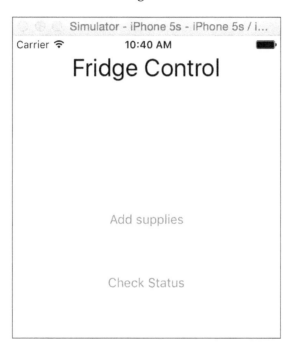

Go to its Swift file and add a method that will allow the other scenes to unwind to the main scene, which is a concept we've already seen in the previous chapters that allows us to return directly to this view controller. Eventually, you can implement this method, but leave it empty right now. Place the following code to create the custom `segue` method:

```
@IBAction func
unwindToInitialViewController(segue:UIStoryboardSegue)
{
}
```

The models

Let's create some models before we start with any visual part for the app. First, add a new file called `Supply.swift`. Here, we are going to create a class that represents some supplies, which can be of the drink, food, and dessert types. To differentiate them, we are going to create an enumeration called `SupplyType`:

```
enum SupplyType:String{
    case Drink = "drink", Food = "food", Dessert = "dessert"
}
```

 You can create enumerations nested in a class; however, this kind of implementations still have some limitations. Therefore, it is still considered to be a better idea while implementing it independently.

Now, we need to create the `Supply` class. In this class, we need an attribute for the supply's name, another one for its type, and two private attributes to control its duration. We will also create a method to consume such supplies and another one to estimate when they are going to end. Remember that their duration is based on the time we need to consume the supply, not on their weight or size:

```
class Supply {
    var name:String
    var type:SupplyType
    private var duration:UInt
    private var consumed:UInt = 0
```

As none of these attributes are optional and not all of them are initialized, we will have to create an initializer. We could declare them with an exclamation mark, but it is not a good practice to abuse it. Copy this code to create the initializer:

```
init(name:String, type:SupplyType, duration:UInt) {
    self.name = name
    self.type = type
    self.duration = duration
}
```

Now, we need to indicate the amount of time that was consumed. If the product was fully consumed, we have to return the amount of time remaining to consume the next product:

```
func consume(seconds: UInt) -> UInt{
    if consumed + seconds > duration {
        let rest:UInt = seconds - (duration - consumed)
        consumed = duration
```

```
        return rest
    }
    consumed += seconds
    return 0
}
```

At last, we have to create a method that indicates how much time is remaining for this supply. We can then close the class:

```
func endEstimation() -> UInt {
    return duration - consumed
}
}
```

Pay attention that, in this class, we used an unsigned integer instead of a signed integer, as there is no sense in mentioning negative time. Bear this decision in mind as it needs to be like this for the whole app.

The second class we have to implement is the fridge. Add a new file called `Fridge.swift` to your project. The fridge will have an instance that can be accessed anywhere and some constants that can control the supplies' lifetime. All these properties are static, as they don't need to be accessed through an instance; you can just call them by calling them through the class. Place the following code to start the class' implementation:

```
class Fridge {
    private static var instance:Fridge?
    #if DEBUG
    // on debug mode 1 day will be 10 seconds
    static let cycleUnit = UInt(10)
    #else
    static let cycleUnit = UInt(60 * 60 * 24)
    #endif
    static let cycleTime = UInt(30)
    static let cycleThreshold = 0.2
```

Sometimes, you might find the words static and class for properties. What's the difference? Both words mean that the property or the method can be accessed directly through the class without the need of any of its instance. However, static is an alias for final class, which means that the property or function can't be overridden. Another detail you have to consider is that classes can be used only with methods and computed properties, but not with stored properties.

With object attributes, we need a dictionary that controls the supplies of each type and an array with the accepted supply types:

```
private var supplies = [SupplyType: [Supply]]()
private let types:[SupplyType] = [.Drink, .Food, .Dessert]
```

Another attribute that we are going to add is a notification dictionary. This dictionary allows us to know whether the user was notified about the supply's shortage:

```
var notified = [SupplyType.Food: false,
    SupplyType.Drink: false,
    SupplyType.Dessert:false]
```

Technically speaking, it is not necessary to create an initializer for this class. However, it is a good idea to initialize the supplies' dictionary for each key. Otherwise, every time we request a key, we will have to check whether its array exists or not:

```
private init(){
    for type in types {
        supplies[type] = [Supply]()
    }
}
```

Now, we need a method to access the instance of our fridge. When this method is called, it needs to check whether the instance is already created. If not, it will have to allocate its memory and initialize it. After this, the method will return `Fridge` instance:

```
class func mainFridge() -> Fridge {
    if Fridge.instance == nil {
        Fridge.instance = Fridge()
    }
    return Fridge.instance!
}
```

Great! Now, we have to implement some methods to control the supplies. First, let's create a method to add supplies to the fridge. Here, we just need to add the argument to the array of supplies and reset the notification for this supply type:

```
func addSupply(supply:Supply){
    supplies[supply.type]?.append(supply)
    self.notified[supply.type] = false
}
```

The next method is the one that denotes the amount of time consumed, so we have to rest it for each supply type:

```
func consume(seconds:UInt){
    for type in types {
        if let currentSupplies = supplies[type] {
            var time = seconds
            for element in currentSupplies {
                time = element.consume(time)
            }
        }
    }
}
```

We will need another method to check the remaining time for a supply type. This method will allow us to know whether the fridge is running out of any kind of supplies. Here, we are going to use the reduce method, which belongs to the array class. The reduce method iterates through each element of the array and returns a value that is sent to the next iteration. In this case, for each element, we will combine its estimation time with the current accumulator that starts with 0. Type the following code to implement the remainingTime function:

```
func remainingTime(supplyType:SupplyType) -> UInt{
    return supplies[supplyType]!.reduce(0, combine: { (sum,
    element) -> UInt in
        return sum + element.endEstimation()
    })
}
```

Now, we need another method to check the percentage of such supplies. Here, we need some clarification when we say that a percentage mean is based on the fridge cycle. If we usually buy supplies every 30 days and we still have 15 days, it will mean that this method will return 50%. If we have supplies for 60 days, it will return 100% (not 200%) as the fridge is full for one cycle. This method will be used to display the current status of the fridge:

```
func cyclePercentageFor(supplyType:SupplyType) -> Float {
    let percentage = Float(self.remainingTime(supplyType)) /
    Float(Fridge.cycleUnit * Fridge.cycleTime)
    if percentage > 1.0 {
        return 1.0
    }
    return percentage
}
```

As you can see, when a supply reaches the end, it is not removed from the supplies' array. The reason is that we might need it in the future, for example, for the statistics of the products that were consumed. But, can it cause any problem? The answer is yes; if it consumes too much memory, we would have to free the unused records. This is the reason we have to create a method called `compress`. As this is the last method for this class, we are also going to close the class:

```
func compress(){
    for key in self.supplies.keys {
        if let _ = supplies[key], _ = supplies[key]!.first{
            while supplies[key]!.count > 0 &&
            supplies[key]!.first!.endEstimation() == 0  {
                supplies[key]!.removeAtIndex(0)
            }
        }
    }
} // fridge end
```

When should we call this method? We have two options, one is every time we consume some supplies and the other one is when the app receives a low memory warning. In this app, we are going to use the second option. To do it, we are going to add the following method to the app's delegate class:

```
func applicationDidReceiveMemoryWarning(application:
UIApplication) {
    Fridge.mainFridge().compress()
}
```

The last model we need is the supermarket. This model will be a very simple one that will store the `supermarket` address and coordinates and will also have only one instance for the whole app.

Now we can create the `supermarket` class. Add a new Swift file called `Supermarket.swift` to the project and create a class with the same name:

```
class Supermarket{
```

We can then add the attributes; in this case, we need the address, the latitude, the longitude, and also a `static` attribute that contains the instance of the supermarket:

```
var address:String?
var latitude:Double?
var longitude:Double?
private static var instance:Supermarket?
```

As we did in the previous class, we have to create a method that will return the instance of the current class. This is all there's to be done for this class, so we can close it:

```
    static func defaultSupermarket() -> Supermarket{
        if Supermarket.instance == nil {
            Supermarket.instance = Supermarket()
        }
        return self.instance!
    }
} // end Supermarket
```

A scene to add supplies

Starting with the option to add supplies, we create a new file in the project called `AddSuppliesViewController.swift`. Start importing `UIKit` and creating a class that inherits from `UIViewController` with the same name as the file. This class will also work with `UIPickerView`, which implies that we have to implement the `UIPickerViewDataSource` and `UIPickerViewDelegate` protocols. We will also need to implement `UITextFieldDelegate`. Leave this class empty for now; don't worry about the compiler errors:

```
class AddSupplyViewController: UIViewController,
UIPickerViewDataSource, UIPickerViewDelegate, UITextFieldDelegate
{
}
```

Return to the storyboard and add a new view controller to it. Connect the `AddSupply` button from the first scene to this new view controller by control-dragging it from the button to the new scene. Update the scene class in its Identity inspector to **AddSupplyViewController** as shown in the following screenshot:

In this scene, we need to set the product name, the product type (drink, food, or dessert), and the product duration. For this scene, we will need four labels, one text field, two buttons, and two picker views. Set the button's titles to Back and Add product and also set the label's titles to ADD SUPPLIES, Product name, Product type, and How long does it last?. Place them in a way that the user understands the order these fields could be set in, like it is shown in the following screenshot:

The easiest command we are going to create is the Back button. Just control-drag the button to the exit symbol on the scene and select the only method that will appear: unwindToInitialViewController.

Set the text field delegate, the picker view's delegate, and the data source to the current view controller. Also, connect the text field and the pickers to their corresponding attribute in the following code:

```
@IBOutlet var productNameTextField: UITextField!
@IBOutlet var productTypePicker: UIPickerView!
@IBOutlet var durationPicker: UIPickerView!
```

Now let's do the same with the **Add product** button. Instead of connecting them to the attributes, we will connect them to their action. We are going to leave this action empty for now:

```
@IBAction func addProductAction(sender: UIButton!) {
}
```

Before we proceed with the code, let's add a border to the pickers (as it is shown in the previous screenshot). The idea behind it is to check whether, during runtime, there is any UI component that is overlapping with the picker. Remember that `UIPickerView` has a large area that is transparent and it can also be resized due to auto layout.

Select one picker, go to its Identity inspector and scroll down to the **User Defined Runtime Attributes** section. This section is basically a table where you can add some custom attributes. Click on its plus sign that is located in the bottom-left corner of the table. A new row will appear; in the first column, you have to type `layer.borderWidth`; in the second column, you have to change the type to `Number`; and in the third column, you have to set its value to `1`.

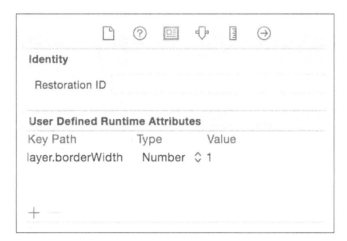

Repeat the same process with the other picker view. Eventually, you can remove these borders if you want to. While the scene is under development, it is a good idea to leave the borders on.

Adding a border to an UI component is one way of knowing the space it is occupying. However, do not forget that a view can have subviews beyond its parent frame. Another way is to use the visual debugger.

Return to the `AddSuppliesViewController.swift` file and continue with its code. Firstly, we have to declare two constant attributes: one that represents the type of supplies displayed by the first picker view and the second one that represents the `durationUnit` type displayed by the second picker. Place the following constants under the current attributes:

```
private let productTypes = ["Drink", "Food", "Dessert"]
private let durationUnit = ["Day", "Week", "Month"]
```

Another attribute that will be necessary is the fridge instance. We could access it by calling the `mainFridge` method every time we need it. But, it is handier if we just create an attribute for it:

```
private let fridge = Fridge.mainFridge()
```

The first methods that we are going to implement are those that belong to the `UIPickerViewDataSource` protocol. This protocol has only two functions and they are mandatory. One is to return the number of components (columns) and the other function is to return the number of elements. They work like the table view delegate. However, the information by itself is not returned by this protocol; it will be returned by the delegate.

The first picker view will have only one component and the second one will have two components: one to the left that displays numbers between 1 and 7 and the one to the right that displays the units (day, week, or month). Type the following code to complete this method:

```
// MARK: - Picker view data source function.
func numberOfComponentsInPickerView(pickerView: UIPickerView)
-> Int{
    if pickerView === self.productTypePicker {
        return 1
    }else {
        return 2
    }
}
```

The next method will tell us the number of rows of a specific component; it also belongs to the UIPickerViewDataSource protocol. In this case, we have three situations. If the app is requesting the number of components for the supply type, it will be the size of the corresponding array. If the app is requesting the size of the other picker view, we have to return the number 7 for the first component or the size of the unit array for the second one. Here, you have the code for the numberOfRowsInComponent method:

```
func pickerView(pickerView: UIPickerView,
numberOfRowsInComponent component: Int) -> Int {
    if pickerView === self.productTypePicker {
        return productTypes.count
    }else {
        return component == 0 ? 7 : self.durationUnit.count
    }
}
```

Now, we have to feed the picker views by implementing the titleForRow method that belongs to UIPickerViewDelegate. Here, we have to return the values of the corresponding arrays or return a number from 1 to 7 in the case of the first component of the duration picker view:

```
// MARK: - Picker view delegate
func pickerView(pickerView: UIPickerView, titleForRow row:
Int, forComponent component: Int) -> String? {
    switch (pickerView, component){
    case (self.productTypePicker, _):
        return productTypes[row]
    case (self.durationPicker, 0):
        return String(row + 1)
    case (self.durationPicker, 1):
        return self.durationUnit[row]
    default:
        return nil
    }
}
```

At this point, you should be able to compile the project with *command + B*. However, we are not finished with this class yet; actually, we haven't even initialized it. To do it, we are going to call a method that will reset the scene. This method will also be called after adding supplies to the fridge and this is the reason we shouldn't code it on the `viewDidLoad` method:

```
override func viewDidLoad() {
    super.viewDidLoad()
    self.setup()
}
func setup(){
    self.productNameTextField.text = ""
    self.productNameTextField.becomeFirstResponder()
    // Food is the default supply
    self.productTypePicker.selectRow(1, inComponent: 0,
    animated: true)
    // 1 day is the default duration
    self.durationPicker.selectRow(0, inComponent: 0, animated:
    true)
    self.durationPicker.selectRow(0, inComponent: 1, animated:
    true)
}
```

The next step is to create a method to add the product on the screen. Firstly, this method needs to check whether the user has introduced any product name, otherwise we will not be able to continue:

```
@IBAction func addProductAction(sender: UIButton!) {
    let name = self.productNameTextField.text!
    if name == "" {
        self.productNameTextField.becomeFirstResponder()
        return
    }
```

Then, we have to check the supply's type. As you can see, there is an extra option that controls some kind of nonexisting selections. It is not really necessary, but it is good to control such an error, as in the future, we could add types of new supplies:

```
let type:SupplyType
switch productTypePicker.selectedRowInComponent(0) {
case 0:
    type = .Drink
case 1:
    type = .Food
case 2:
    type = .Dessert
```

```
default:
    fatalError("Wrong index
    \(productTypePicker.selectedRowInComponent(0)) on file
    \(__FILE__) near line \(__LINE__)")
}
```

We should have the same procedure with the supply period:

```
let period:UInt
switch durationPicker.selectedRowInComponent(1){
case 0:
    period = 1
case 1:
    period = 7
case 2:
    period = 30
default:
    fatalError("Wrong index
    \(productTypePicker.selectedRowInComponent(0)) on file
    \(__FILE__) near line \(__LINE__)")
}
```

Once we have the information on the screen, we can create the supply object and add it to the fridge:

```
let duration =
UInt(self.durationPicker.selectedRowInComponent(0) + 1) *
period * Fridge.cycleUnit
let supply = Supply(name: name, type: type, duration:
duration)
self.fridge.addSupply(supply)
```

Finally, we can just reset the screen and finish this method:

```
        self.setup()
    }
```

Do we still need to do anything in this class? Theoretically no, but in practice, we still need to add one more detail. Once the user types the product name, the keyboard needs to be hidden. So, when the user presses the *Enter* key, the keyboard must be dismissed. We can then close the class:

```
    // MARK: - Text field delegates
    func textFieldShouldReturn(textField: UITextField) -> Bool{
        textField.resignFirstResponder()
        return true
    }
} // end AddSuppliesViewController
```

Displaying the fridge's status

Once we are able to add stuff to our fridge, we need to create another scene to display the current fridge's status. In this scene, we are going to use `UIProgressView` because it is more visual than just writing a number on a label.

Go back to the storyboard and add a new view controller to it. Drag five labels, two buttons, and three progress views to the scene as follows.

1. Place the first label at the top and set its title to `Fridge Status`.

2. Place the second label under the first one without a title or, if you prefer, you can just add a dash to locate it easily. This label will be used to report to the user the supplies that are running out of stock.

3. Under the message label, place one button and set its title to `Go to the supermarket`.

4. You can place the other three labels with a progress view under each one. Set the labels' title to `Drink`, `Food`, and `Dessert`.

5. Lastly, place the second button at the bottom of the scene and set its title to **Back**.

In the end, you should have a layout similar to the following screenshot:

Now, add a new file called `FridgeStatusViewController.swift` and open it. Start by importing the `UIKit` and the `CoreLocation` frameworks. The second framework is necessary, as we will be retrieving the coordinates using `CLGeocoder` afterwards:

```
import UIKit
import CoreLocation
```

Create the `FridgeStatusViewController` class that must inherit from `UIViewController` and add the following UI attributes:

```
class FridgeStatusViewController: UIViewController {
    @IBOutlet var goToTheSupermarketButton: UIButton!
    @IBOutlet var statusLabel: UILabel!
    @IBOutlet var drinkBar: UIProgressView!
    @IBOutlet var foodBar: UIProgressView!
    @IBOutlet var dessertBar: UIProgressView!
```

Another attribute that is necessary is the `fridge` instance. This one can be a constant, as we don't have two instances of `fridge` in this app:

```
let fridge = Fridge.mainFridge()
```

The next step is to create the `viewDidLoad` method to initialize the visual part. Firstly, we are going to create an array variable called `lowLevel`, which will store the supplies that are being depleted. Type the following code to start the `viewDidLoad` method:

```
override func viewDidLoad() {
    super.viewDidLoad()
    var lowLevel = [String]()
```

Now, we can set the supplies' progress view and append the needed values to `lowLevel`:

```
        let drinkPercentage = fridge.cyclePercentageFor(.Drink)
        drinkBar.progress = drinkPercentage
        if drinkPercentage <= 0.2 {
            lowLevel.append(SupplyType.Drink.rawValue)
        }

        let foodPercentage = fridge.cyclePercentageFor(.Food)
        foodBar.progress = foodPercentage
        if foodPercentage <= 0.2 {
            lowLevel.append(SupplyType.Food.rawValue)
        }

        let dessertPercentage =
        fridge.cyclePercentageFor(.Dessert)
```

```
dessertBar.progress = dessertPercentage
if dessertPercentage <= 0.2 {
    lowLevel.append(SupplyType.Dessert.rawValue)
}
```

The last part of this method is to set the status label. Here, we have three cases:

- When there is no food at all, we should report that the fridge is completely empty. In this case, we should display the button that shows the route to the supermarket.

- When there is enough amount of each supply, we will report it and hide the `supermarket` button.

- When there are some supplies that are being depleted, we will report the supplies that need attention and the `supermarket` button should be displayed.

Place this code to complete the `viewDidLoad` method:

```
if drinkPercentage == 0 &&
    foodPercentage == 0 &&
    dessertPercentage == 0 {
        statusLabel.text = "The fridge is empty!!"
        goToTheSupermarketButton.hidden = false
}else if lowLevel.count == 0 {
        statusLabel.text = "The fridge has enough
        supplies"
    goToTheSupermarketButton.hidden = true
}else {
    let join = lowLevel.joinWithSeparator(", ")
    statusLabel.text = "The fridge is running out of:
    \(join)"
    goToTheSupermarketButton.hidden = false
}
}
```

The next and the last method of this view controller is called `goToTheSupermarket`, which will check whether the supermarket has the address with its coordinates set. Then, it will open a scene with the map and the directions to get there. We start by creating a nested function that opens the map's scene, as this code will be used more than once:

```
@IBAction func goToTheSupermarket(sender: UIButton) {
    let supermarket = Supermarket.defaultSupermarket()
    func openMap(){
```

```
        let mapviewcontroller =
self.storyboard!.
instantiateViewControllerWithIdentifier("supermarketviewcontroller")
        self.presentViewController(mapviewcontroller,
        animated: true, completion: nil)
    }
```

Then, we check whether the supermarket's address is set. If so, we will just call the openMap function:

```
    if let _ = supermarket.address {
        openMap()
    }
```

If no address is set, we will have to create an alert controller with a text field to write the address with the following code:

```
    else {
        let alertController = UIAlertController(title:
        "Address not found", message: "There is no supermarket
        address set, please introduce it.", preferredStyle:
        .Alert)
    alertController.addTextFieldWithConfigurationHandler(nil)
```

Once the alert controller is created, we have to create its actions. The first action is to get the content of the text field and find its coordinates using a geocoder object. Once it is located, we can set the corresponding values to the supermarket object and open the map:

```
        let acceptAction = UIAlertAction(title: "Ok", style:
        .Default, handler: { (action) -> Void in
            let address:String =
            alertController.textFields![0].text!
            let geocoder = CLGeocoder()
            geocoder.geocodeAddressString(address,
            completionHandler: { (placemarks:[CLPlacemark]?,
            error:NSError?) -> Void in
                if let error = error {
                    print(error.localizedDescription)
                }
                if let placemarks = placemarks where
                placemarks.count > 0 {
                    supermarket.address = address
                    supermarket.latitude =
                    placemarks[0].location!.coordinate.latitude
```

```
                         supermarket.longitude =
                         placemarks[0].location!.coordinate.longitude
                         openMap()
                   }
             })
        })
        alertController.addAction(acceptAction)
```

The second action is to just create the `Cancel` button; it means that all we have to do is to create an empty action and add it to the alert controller:

```
        let cancelAction = UIAlertAction(title: "Cancel",
        style: .Cancel, handler: nil)
        alertController.addAction(cancelAction)
```

Finally, we can present the alert controller and close the brackets till we close the class:

```
        self.presentViewController(alertController, animated:
        true, completion: nil)
      } // end else
    } // end goToSupermarket method
  }// end FridgeStatusViewController class
```

Great! The code for this class is ready. Return to the storyboard, update the view controller class to `FridgeStatusViewController`, and connect the visual parts to the corresponding attributes. Don't forget that the **Back** button must be connected to the `unwindToInitialViewController` method that will return to the `InitialViewController` method.

Test the current app's status by adding some supplies and checking their statuses. The only feature that can't be tested now is the `supermarket` button, otherwise your app will crash.

Going to the supermarket

Now, it is time to create the last scene of the iOS app. Here, we just need to add a new view controller with a label, map view, table view, and button to the storyboard.

A label is used only to display the scene's title. Therefore, we will set its title to Supermarket Directions and place it at the top of the screen. Then, we will place the map under it to occupy approximately half the screen. Below the map, we will place the table view; here is where will display the directions. Lastly, we will place the button with the Main Menu title. The final layout should be similar to the following screenshot:

Add a new file to your project called MapViewController.swift and import the UIKit, MapKit, and CoreLocation frameworks with the following code:

```
import UIKit
import MapKit
import CoreLocation
```

Create the corresponding class by calling it `MapViewController`, inheriting from `UIViewController` and implementing the `MKMapViewDelegate` and `UITableViewDataSource` protocols:

```
class MapViewController:UIViewController, MKMapViewDelegate,
UITableViewDataSource {
```

As usual, we are going to start by adding its attributes. First, we need the map instance and the table view instance:

```
@IBOutlet var mapView: MKMapView!
@IBOutlet var stepsTableView: UITableView!
```

The next attributes are an array of `MKRouteStep` that represents the directions to the supermarket, and `locationManager` that will request permission to use the GPS:

```
var steps:[MKRouteStep]?
let locationManager = CLLocationManager()
```

After we create the attributes, we are going to implement the `viewDidLoad` method by telling the location manager to request for authorization and receive updates:

```
override func viewDidLoad() {
    super.viewDidLoad()

    locationManager.requestWhenInUseAuthorization()
    locationManager.startUpdatingLocation()
```

Then, we can retrieve information from the supermarket to create its map item. This map item will be used to set our destination on the map:

```
let supermarket = Supermarket.defaultSupermarket()
let coordinate =
CLLocationCoordinate2DMake(supermarket.latitude!,
supermarket.longitude!)
let placemark = MKPlacemark(coordinate: coordinate,
addressDictionary: nil)
let destination = MKMapItem(placemark: placemark)
destination.name = "Supermarket"
```

Once we have our destination, we can create a request by creating an object of the `MKDirectionsRequest` type. This object needs to know the source, the destination, and the transport type, which for this app will be by car. In this case, we are not going to accept alternative routes:

```
let request = MKDirectionsRequest()
request.source = MKMapItem.mapItemForCurrentLocation()
print(MKMapItem.mapItemForCurrentLocation())
```

```
request.destination = destination
request.transportType = .Automobile
request.requestsAlternateRoutes = false
```

To finish this method, let's create an object of the `MKDirections` type and tell it to calculate the directions. Once it gets the directions, we have to update the maps with a route overlay and update the table view with the directions:

```
let directions = MKDirections(request: request)
directions.calculateDirectionsWithCompletionHandler({(response:
    MKDirectionsResponse?, error: NSError?) in
    if let error = error {
        print(error.localizedDescription)
    } else {
        let route = response!.routes[0]
        self.mapView.addOverlay(route.polyline,
            level: MKOverlayLevel.AboveRoads)
        self.steps = route.steps
        self.stepsTableView.reloadData()
    }
})
}
```

Curiously, adding the overlay is not enough for it to be displayed. We still need to implement the `renderForOverlay` method and set the line color and width:

```
func mapView(mapView: MKMapView, rendererForOverlay overlay:
MKOverlay) -> MKOverlayRenderer {
    let renderer = MKPolylineRenderer(overlay: overlay)
    renderer.strokeColor = UIColor.blueColor()
    renderer.lineWidth = 5.0
    return renderer
}
```

Now we can implement the table view data source methods. For `numberOfRowsInSection`, we have two possibilities. The first one is to return the number of elements to the steps array and the second one is to return `nil` when the arrays aren't set yet:

```
func tableView(tableView: UITableView, numberOfRowsInSection
section: Int) -> Int{
    if let steps = self.steps {
        return steps.count
    }
    return 0
}
```

The last method is `cellForRowAtIndexPath`. Here, we just need to create a table cell and set its text to the value of the instructions attribute of the corresponding step:

```
func tableView(tableView: UITableView, cellForRowAtIndexPath
indexPath: NSIndexPath) -> UITableViewCell {
    var cell =
tableView.dequeueReusableCellWithIdentifier("cell")
    if cell == nil {
        cell = UITableViewCell(style: .Default,
        reuseIdentifier: "cell")
    }
    cell?.textLabel?.text =
    self.steps?[indexPath.row].instructions
    return cell!
}
} // end MapViewController
```

The code for this class is ready. Now, we will return to the storyboard and control-drag the table view to the view controller icon (yellow circle with a white square inside) to set its delegate. Repeat the same procedure with **Map View**. Once both the delegates are set, select the map view, go to its attribute inspector, and check the option that shows the **User Location**, as shown in the following screenshot:

Now, click on the view controller, update its class to **MapViewController** on the Identity inspector, and set **Storyboard ID** to `supermarketviewcontroller`, as shown in the following screenshot:

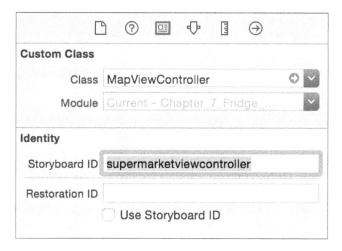

There is still one small detail to be done; click on the iOS app's `info.plist` file, add one record with the **NSLocationWhenInUseUsageDescription** key, and set its value to **This app needs your location for routing you to the supermarket**. This step is mandatory since iOS 8 and remember that this app is done for watchOS 2, which requires iOS 9 or above.

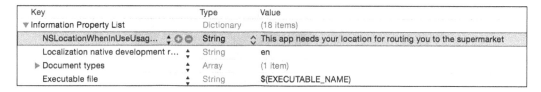

Test the app again and you should be able to see the maps with the directions to your supermarket.

You can simulate pinching with two fingers to zoom in and zoom out on the simulator by using the mouse with the option key pressed. If you need to place the fingers location at a different place, you can move them with *option + shift*.

The WatchApp

Once the iOS app is almost ready (we still need to return here for a few details), we can go to the WatchKit app. Before we start coding, we are going to add a few resources to our project. First, we will add the `drink.png`, `food.png`, `dessert.png`, and `status*.png` images that can be found in the book resource to the WatchKit app.

 These radio images are very popular on Watch Apps. You can customize and download them from `http://hmaidasani.github.io/RadialChartImageGenerator/`. There are options to change the image size, remove text on the screen, and change the line's colors.

Click on the storyboard that is now located in the `Chapter 7 Fridge Control WatchKit App` group. Here, you can see that we have some default scenes. One of them is the scene that represents the app, which has its initial arrow marked with the word **Main**. Click on this scene and double-click on the top portion next to the clock to set the scene title. When the text field appears, type `Fridge Control` as shown in the following screenshot:

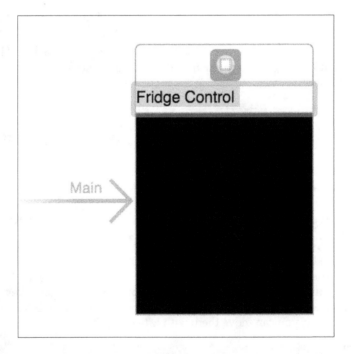

Drag a table to this scene. Note that the table has a different aspect than the one we know on the iOS app. Don't worry about it for now; just drag an image and a label to the only row we have, as we are going to customize the row.

Click on the image and go to its attribute inspector (*command* + *option* + *4*). Go to the section titled **Size** and change its width type to **Fixed** and set its value to **32**.

Now, click on the label, move it to right of the image if it is not there yet, and change its **Horizontal** and **Vertical** alignment to **Center**.

The layout of this scene is basically ready, but we still need to create a class that will represent our cell (or row as it is called here). Add a new file to the project called `SupplyRow.swift`; but this time, before we press the **Create** button in the file dialog, we will have to ensure this file belongs to the `Chapter 7 Fridge Control WatchKit Extension` group and its target is the WatchKit Extension, as it is shown in the following sample:

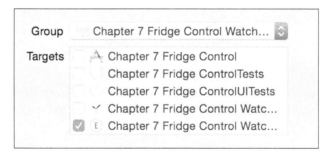

In this file, we just need to create a simple class that inherits from `NSObject` (yes, a row here is `NSObject`) and contains `WKInterfaceImage` and `WKInterfaceLabel`, which are the equivalent of `UIImageView` and `UILabel` on the watch:

```
import WatchKit
class SupplyRow:NSObject {
    @IBOutlet var image:WKInterfaceImage!
    @IBOutlet var caption:WKInterfaceLabel!
}
```

Return to the WatchApp storyboard and select **Table Row Controller** on the Document Outline, as shown in the following screenshot:

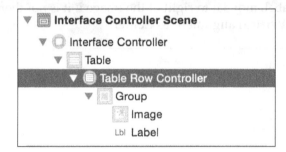

Go to the Identity inspector and update the **Class** type to **SupplyRow**, which is the class name that we have just created.

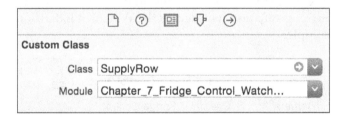

We then need to set the **Identifier** field that is located on the attribute inspector. This field is important as, in the code, we have to call the value that was set. In this case, we are going to set it to `supplyrow`.

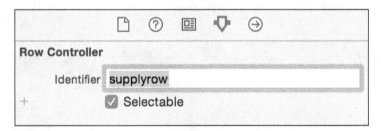

Now, you can link the image and the label to their corresponding attributes by going to the connections inspector and dragging the plus signs to the UI components.

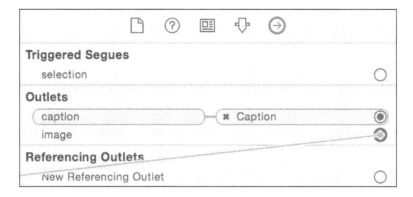

Now, we need to create another class to store the nonvisual information of each row. This class will be used to exchange information between controllers. It will be called `RowInfo` and it will store the title visible to the user, the image name, and the corresponding raw value for the supply type.

Add a new file called `RowInfo.swift` to the Watch extension. Create one class with the same name, and three string attributes. Then, create an initializer that sets the attributes' initial values. The code is as follows:

```
class RowInfo {
    var title:String
    var image:String
    var key:String

    init(title:String, image:String, key:String){
        self.title = title
        self.image = image
        self.key = key
    }
}
```

The previous class is not a tuple, as the instance of its objects are going to be sent from one interface controller to another as contexts that must be an instance of the `AnyObject` type.

Now you can go to the `InterfaceController.swift` file. As you can see here, the class inherits from `WKInterfaceController` that is equivalent to `UIViewController`. Bear it in mind as the methods here are different.

In this class, we will need two attributes: the first one is the table instance that is WKInterfaceTable here, and another one that is an array of RowInfo:

```
class InterfaceController: WKInterfaceController {
    @IBOutlet var statusTable: WKInterfaceTable!
    var rowsInfo = [RowInfo]()
```

Now, let's implement the awakeWithContext method that is created to initialize the attributes, something similar to viewDidLoad. Here, we have to start by creating the elements of the RowInfo array:

```
override func awakeWithContext(context: AnyObject?) {
    super.awakeWithContext(context)
    var rowInfo = RowInfo(title: "Drink", image:  "drink",
    key: "drink")
    rowsInfo.append(rowInfo)
    rowInfo = RowInfo(title: "Food", image: "food", key:
    "food")
    rowsInfo.append(rowInfo)
    rowInfo = RowInfo(title: "Dessert", image: "dessert", key:
    "dessert")
    rowsInfo.append(rowInfo)
```

Now we can initialize the table's elements. In iOS table views, we have to use the numberOfRowsInSection and cellForItemAtIndexPath methods. However, WKInterfaceTable works in a different way. We have to set the rows together with the setNumberOfRows method, where we tell the number of rows and its type, as shown in the following code:

```
statusTable.setNumberOfRows(rowsInfo.count, withRowType:
"supplyrow")
```

Then, we can iterate through each retrieved row to set its contents. The rowControllerAtIndex method returns the corresponding object of a row and, with it, we can set up this cell. Copying the following loop code will set the rows and close the method:

```
for i in 0..<statusTable.numberOfRows {
    let row = statusTable.rowControllerAtIndex(i) as!
    SupplyRow
    let rowInfo = rowsInfo[i]
    row.caption.setText(rowInfo.title)
    let image = UIImage(named: rowInfo.title)
    row.image.setImage(image)
}
}
```

Now, the first watch scene is done and ready to be tested. To do it, select the watch app on the combo scheme as shown in the following screenshot and select your favorite simulator or device. Remember that, if you have a physical device, it must be paired with the phone. The app will first be installed on the phone and then sent to the watch. This process could take a while at times.

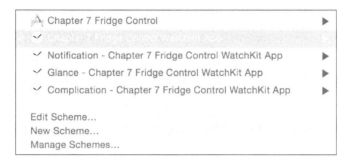

When the simulator appears, you should have two windows, one for the iPhone simulator and another one for the watch simulator. The final result should be a window as shown in the following screenshot:

While developing watch apps, test them with both the models: 38 mm and 42 mm. If you have a physical device, test on it, so you can have a more accurate result.

Communicating with the iOS app

Once the user has chosen the supply type, the app should display the supply status. However, this information is not on the watch, it is on the phone; it must be requested using a framework called `WatchConnectivity`.

This new scene will display the current supply status of the supply. If the user has set the `supermarket` address, a button will appear to display the map with the `supermarket` address.

Go to the WatchApp storyboard and add a new interface controller next to the first one. Drag a label, an image, and a button to this interface controller. Select the label and change its text alignment to center and its width size to **Relative to Container** with its value as **1**, as shown in the following screenshot:

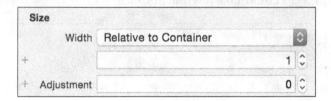

Now, click on the image and set its **Horizontal** and **Vertical** alignment to **Center**. Change the **Width** and **Height** size to **Fixed** and set their values to **80**, as it is displayed in the following screenshot:

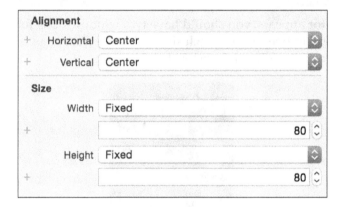

Now, click on the button, set its text to Supermarket, its **Vertical** alignment to **Bottom**, and its **Horizontal** alignment to **Center**. It is also useful to display the text Return on the top of the screen next to the < symbol. This way, users will know that by double-clicking on it, they will return to the main menu.

The last visual work we have to do here is creating a segue that connects the first scene with this one. Control-drag from the table of the first scene to this new scene. Now your layout should be similar to this one.

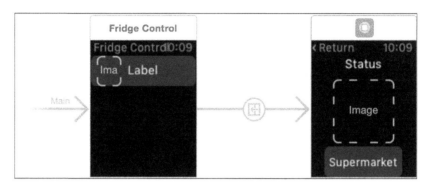

Select the new segue by clicking on its arrow and go to its attribute inspector. Set its identifier to supplysegue. This step is not essential for this app, but it might be for any other watch app that you would develop. It is also a good idea to identify segues in terms of software maintenance.

Now return to the InterfaceController.swift file. Here, we are going to add a new method to send the corresponding user selection to the next scene. This method is called contextForSegueWithIdentifier and it is similar to prepareForSegue in the iOS app. We just need to return the object that would be sent as an argument to the awakeWithContext method of the next scene. Place the following code in the InterfaceController class:

```
override func contextForSegueWithIdentifier(segueIdentifier:
String, inTable table: WKInterfaceTable, rowIndex: Int) ->
AnyObject? {
    if segueIdentifier == "supplysegue" {
        return rowsInfo[rowIndex]
    }
    return nil
}
```

Now we can code the next interface controller's class. Add a new file called `SupplyStatusInterfaceController.swift` to the Watch Extension target. Start by importing the `WatchKit` and the `WatchConnectivity` frameworks with the following code:

```
import WatchKit
import WatchConnectivity
```

Next, we have to open the class by calling it `SupplyStatusInterfaceController`, inheriting from `WKInterfaceController` and specifying that it follows the `WCSessionDelegate` protocol:

```
class SupplyStatusInterfaceController: WKInterfaceController,
WCSessionDelegate {
```

We are going to create an attribute for each UI component we place in the scene:

```
@IBOutlet var statusLabel: WKInterfaceLabel!
@IBOutlet var statusImage: WKInterfaceImage!
@IBOutlet var supermarketButton: WKInterfaceButton!
```

Besides these attributes, we still need an attribute that will contain the `supermarket` location, which will be implemented with a dictionary. Add another attribute, that is, a `rowInfo` object that contains the user selection in the previous scene:

```
var supermarketData:[String:AnyObject]?
var rowInfo:RowInfo!
```

Now, we can start initializing the interface controller by creating the `awakeWithContext` method. Firstly, we have to convert the argument from `AnyObject` to `RowInfo` and assign it to our `rowInfo` attribute. We can then set the scene title:

```
override func awakeWithContext(context: AnyObject?) {
    super.awakeWithContext(context)
    self.rowInfo = context as! RowInfo
    statusLabel.setText("\(rowInfo.title) Status")
}
```

Every time this screen appears, we are going to refresh its data. To do it, we need to communicate with the phone. This process is done by using an object of the `WCSession` type. Place the following code to initialize the session:

```
override func didAppear() {
    let session = WCSession.defaultSession()
    session.delegate = self
    session.activateSession()
```

Now, we need to check whether the phone is reachable or not. Remember that it can be far away from the watch or could be turned off, for example:

```
if session.reachable {
```

If the phone is reachable, we have to send a dictionary that represents our request. For this first message, we are going to send the `"status"` value for one key called `"request"`, and a `rowInfo` key for another dictionary key called `"type"`. None of these attributes are specified by Apple; it is just a convention we have for this app.

When the phone replies, we are going to receive another dictionary with the current status' value. Remember that this value is a `Float` type (like 0.45); we need to multiply it by 100 and convert it to `Int` (like 45 instead of 0.45). Once we have the current percentage, we can call the corresponding image with its full filename, like `status45.png` for example:

```
session.sendMessage(["request":"status",
    "type":rowInfo.key],
    replyHandler: { (reply) -> Void in
        // Handle reply
        dispatch_async(dispatch_get_main_queue(), { () ->
        Void in
            let percentage = Int(reply["value"] as! Float
            * 100.0)
            self.statusImage.setImageNamed("status\
(percentage)")
        })
    },
    errorHandler: { (error) -> Void in
        // Handle error
        print(error.localizedDescription)

})
```

Now, we can do a similar process to request the `supermarket` data. In this case, if the returned value is empty, we are going to hide the `supermarket` button. But if it is not, we are going to store its data in the `supermarketData` attribute and display the button:

```
session.sendMessage(["request":"supermarket"],
    replyHandler: { (reply) -> Void in
        // Handle reply
        dispatch_async(dispatch_get_main_queue(), { () ->
        Void in
            if let value = reply["value"] as?
            [String:AnyObject]{
```

```
                    self.supermarketData = value
                    self.supermarketButton.setHidden(false)
                }else {
                    self.supermarketButton.setHidden(true)
                }
            })
        },
        errorHandler: { (error) -> Void in
            // Handle error
            print(error.localizedDescription)
        })
    }
```

Finally, we can create the method that will send the information to the next scene (the map scene). As it was mentioned before, this method is called `contextForSegueWithIdentifier`. But this time, it has fewer arguments, as it is not going to be called from a table. After this method, we can close the class:

```
override func contextForSegueWithIdentifier(segueIdentifier:
String) -> AnyObject? {
    if segueIdentifier == "mapsegue" {
        return self.supermarketData
    }
    return nil
}
} // end SupplyStatusInterfaceController class
```

Return to the storyboard and click on the last interface controller we created. Go to its Identity inspector and update **Class** to `SupplyStatusInterfaceController`, as shown in the following screenshot:

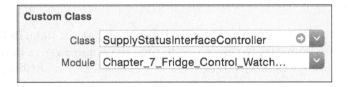

Connect the label, image, and button to their corresponding attributes. You may ask yourself whether you can test the app now. The answer is no! We still need to update the iOS part that receives requests and replies to them.

Go to the `AppDelegate.swift` file of the iOS app and import the `WatchConnectivity` framework:

```
import WatchConnectivity
```

Next, specify that the app delegate will follow the `WCSessionDelegate` protocol by appending the following highlighted code:

```
class AppDelegate: UIResponder, UIApplicationDelegate,
WCSessionDelegate{
```

Using the `didFinishLaunchingWithOptions` method, we are going to get the default session, set its delegate, and activate it. So, the final code of this method should be as follows:

```
func application(application: UIApplication,
didFinishLaunchingWithOptions launchOptions: [NSObject:
AnyObject]?) -> Bool {

    let session = WCSession.defaultSession()
    session.delegate = self
    session.activateSession()

    return true
}
```

Now, we have to append the `didReceiveMessage` method, which belongs to the `WCSessionDelegate` class, to the `AppDelegate` class. This method will start by checking whether the request has a key called `"request"`. In this case, we can reply to the watch app:

```
@available(iOS 9.0, *)
func session(session: WCSession, didReceiveMessage message:
[String : AnyObject], replyHandler: ([String : AnyObject]) ->
Void){
    if let request = message["request"] as? String {
```

If the request is for the fridge's `status` information, we just need to request `fridge` for it and reply with the handler that was sent by the argument:

```
switch request{
case "status":
    let fridge = Fridge.mainFridge()
    let type = message["type"] as! String
    let status =
fridge.cyclePercentageFor(SupplyType(rawValue: type)!)
    replyHandler(["response": "status",
        "value": status])
```

If the request is for the `supermarket` data, we are going to create a new dictionary and return the `address`, `latitude`, and `longitude`. However, if the `supermarket` address is not set, we are just going to reply that the information is not available:

```
case "supermarket":
    let supermarket = Supermarket.defaultSupermarket()
    if let address = supermarket.address,
        latitude = supermarket.latitude,
        longitude = supermarket.longitude {
            replyHandler(["response": "supermarket",
                "value":["address": address,
                "latitude": latitude,
                "longitude": longitude]])
    }else {
        replyHandler(["response": "unavailable"])
    }
```

Lastly, we need to create a default option and return that the request was not found. Then, we can close the method:

```
default:
    replyHandler(["response": "notfound"])
}// end switch
}// end if
} // end didReceiveMessage
```

Now it is time to test the app. You should see the status circle. If you set the address on the iOS app, you should see the **Supermarket** button appear.

Displaying the map on the watch

The last part of our watch app and extension is to display the map to the supermarket. To do it, we are going to use the `WKInterfaceMap` class that is the watch version of `UIMapView`.

Return to the watch storyboard and add a new interface controller. Start by changing the title at the top of the screen to `Return`, so it would be easier for the user to understand how to return to the previous screen.

Place a map on this interface controller and set its width and height to **Relative to Container** with the value to **1**, as shown in the following screenshot:

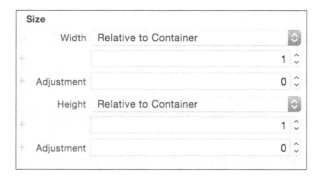

Now, add a new file named `MapController.swift` to the watch extension. Import the `WatchKit` framework and open the class that inherits from `WKInterfaceController`:

```
import WatchKit

class MapController: WKInterfaceController {
```

In this class, we will need two attributes, the map itself and the `supermarket` data that was sent from the previous interface controller:

```
@IBOutlet var map: WKInterfaceMap!
var supermarketData:[String:AnyObject]!
```

Now, we can initialize the `supermarketData` attribute by assigning the context argument sent on the `awakeWithContext` method to it:

```
override func awakeWithContext(context: AnyObject?) {
    self.supermarketData = context as! [String:AnyObject]
}
```

After this, we can implement the `willActivate` method that is equivalent to `viewWillAppear` of `UIViewController`. Here, we just need to add a map annotation (a purple pin in this case) with the `supermarket` coordinates and set its region, which means that we are basically setting the zoom level. That's all for this class, so don't forget to close it:

```
override func willActivate() {
    let latitude = self.supermarketData["latitude"] as! Double
    let longitude = self.supermarketData["longitude"] as!
    Double
```

```
        let location = CLLocationCoordinate2D(latitude: latitude,
        longitude: longitude)
        map.addAnnotation(location, withPinColor: .Purple)
        let region = MKCoordinateRegion(center: location, span:
MKCoordinateSpan(latitudeDelta: 0.005, longitudeDelta: 0.005))
        self.map.setRegion(region)
    }
} // end MapController
```

Return to the WatchApp storyboard, update the interface controller class to `MapController`, and connect the map to the corresponding attribute. Then, control-drag the `supermarket` button of the previous scene to this interface controller. Select the segue and set its identifier to `mapsegue`.

Now you can test the app. Set the `supermarket` address on the iOS app and check whether it appears on the WatchApp. It is interesting to see that if you tap on the watch map, it will open the maps application.

The glance

The glance is a screen that appears when you swipe from the bottom to the top of your watch when the time is being displayed. It is like a single-screen application.

Go to the WatchApp storyboard and check whether there is an interface controller with an initial arrow that has the word **Glance** on it. By default, we have two groups in this interface controller. Drag one label to the group at the top and set its title to `Fridge Status`. Click on the second group, go to its attribute inspector, and change its **Layout** value from **Horizontal** to **Vertical**, as shown in the following screenshot:

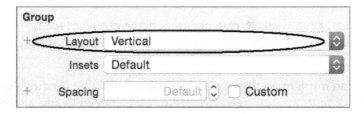

Now drag three labels to this group. These labels should be connected to the following attributes that we will have to type in the `GlanceController.swift` class:

```
@IBOutlet var drinkLabel: WKInterfaceLabel!
@IBOutlet var foodLabel: WKInterfaceLabel!
@IBOutlet var dessertLabel: WKInterfaceLabel!
```

We are then going to complete the `GlanceController` class. First, we are going to import the `WatchConnectivity` framework:

```
import WatchConnectivity
```

Then, we are going to assign the `WCSessionDelegate` framework to the `GlanceController` class:

```
class GlanceController: WKInterfaceController, WCSessionDelegate {
```

Now, inside the class, get the session as we did for WatchApp. Set its delegate to the current object and activate the session:

```
override func willActivate() {
    // This method is called when watch view controller is
    about to be visible to user
    super.willActivate()
    if (WCSession.isSupported()) {
        let session = WCSession.defaultSession()
        session.delegate = self
        session.activateSession()
```

Next, we can send a message to the watch, requesting for the percentage of drinks. When the reply is called, we just have to update `drinkLabel`:

```
session.sendMessage(["request":"status",
"type":"drink"],
    replyHandler: { (reply) -> Void in
        dispatch_async(dispatch_get_main_queue(), { ()
        -> Void in
            let percentage = Int(reply["value"] as!
            Float * 100.0)
            self.drinkLabel.setText("Drink
            \(percentage)%")
        })
    },
    errorHandler: { (error) -> Void in
        print(error.localizedDescription)
})
```

We just need to repeat the same code for the food and dessert and the method is ready:

```
session.sendMessage(["request":"status",
"type":"food"],
    replyHandler: { (reply) -> Void in
        dispatch_async(dispatch_get_main_queue(), { ()
        -> Void in
```

```
                              let percentage = Int(reply["value"] as!
                              Float * 100.0)
                              self.foodLabel.setText("Food
                              \(percentage)%")
                      })
                  },
                  errorHandler: { (error) -> Void in
                      print(error.localizedDescription)
              })

          session.sendMessage(["request":"status",
          "type":"dessert"],
              replyHandler: { (reply) -> Void in
                  dispatch_async(dispatch_get_main_queue(), { ()
                  -> Void in
                      let percentage = Int(reply["value"] as!
                      Float * 100.0)
                      self.dessertLabel.setText("Dessert
                      \(percentage)%")
                  })
              },
              errorHandler: { (error) -> Void in
                  print(error.localizedDescription)
          })
      }
  }
```

Great! The app is ready. Change the scheme to glance and test it.

Summary

In this chapter, we had a different app this time, we had to create an app for Apple Watch. As you could see, creating an Apple Watch app implies that you need to create an iOS app.

Our iOS app worked as the heart of our app; it could set up the fridge and set the supermarket address and tasks that were not done on the watch as there was no keyboard on it. We could also retrieve directions to the supermarket, display them in a table view, and draw the route on the map.

Technically speaking, the Watch app is split into two parts: the extension, which contains the code and some resources needed by the code; and the app, which contains the storyboard and some resources.

In this app, we had to work with classes that were different from the traditional `UIKit` framework. We used `WKInterfaceController` instead of `UIViewController`, `WKInterfaceTable` instead of `UITableView`, `WKIgnterfaceImage` instead of `UIImageView`, and so on.

watchOS 2 brings a new way to exchange information between the watch and iPhone. It is called the **Watch Communication** framework, and we could use it to request and reply.

The final feature we saw was glance. This feature allowed us to check the fridge's status very fast, as we didn't have to open the app itself. We just had to open the glances that were like single `WKInterfaceController` framework and search for the corresponding one.

In the next chapter, you will learn how to edit an existing video using `AVFoundation`, which is a low-level framework designed to manipulate audios and videos.

8
AVFoundation

As mentioned in the previous chapters, smartphones have replaced cameras. Nowadays, it is very common to take pictures or record videos and upload them on websites such as Facebook or Youtube.

Using `UIImagePickerController` can be enough if you just need to take a photo or record a simple video. However, there are times when you need to do more advanced tasks. `UIImagePickerController` is not enough to work with low level media manipulation. To do it, you need to use the AVFoundation framework.

In this chapter, we are going to create an app where the user will take an existing video and replace its sound with a narrative.

In this chapter, we will cover:

- Playing a video with AVFoundation
- Audio recording
- Working with temporary files
- Querying with the `Photos` framework
- Merging assets

Getting a project overview

In this chapter, we are going to create a new app that will make a fusion of a video with an audio. This will allow us to select a video and replace its audio with our narrative. Imagine that you have a video with some landscapes and you would like to replace the current audio with your narrative. That's the idea of this app.

To the user, it will look like he/she is recording over the video, but technically speaking, the user is recording his/her voice on an independent file while watching the video. The merging will be done afterwards.

This app will use AVFoundation and other additional frameworks such as Photos and Core Motion.

Setting up the app

Open your Xcode and create a new single-view application as usual. In the dialog that asks for the project's options, set the application's name to Chapter 8 Rehash; also, ensure that **Swift** is the default language. The final dialog setup should be like the following screenshot:

Rename the ViewController.swift file as well as its class to InitialViewController.swift. Go to the storyboard and update the scene view controller to InitialViewController, as shown in the following screenshot:

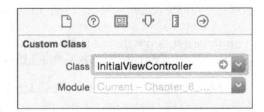

Storing some asset information

Before we start with the scenes, we must create a class that will store some information about the files that are being used for our media edition. Add a new Swift file to our project and call it `AssetInfo.swift`. Start importing `UIKit`, as it is shown in the next line, because we are going to use the `UIImage` class:

```
import UIKit
```

Open the class by calling it `AssetInfo`; it won't inherit from any specific class or implement any protocol. So, its header must be simple, as follows:

```
class AssetInfo {
```

Now, we can start with the first attribute, that is the video thumbnail image. Add the following attribute to your class:

```
var videoThumbnail:UIImage?
```

Besides the video thumbnail, we also need to store the video date and its corresponding URL. Both the attributes are mandatory as the date will be some kind of title and, without the video URL, we won't be able to open it. Place the following attributes and the initializer in your `AssetInfo` class:

```
var videoDate:String
var videoUrl:NSURL

init(videoDate:String, videoUrl:NSURL){
    self.videoDate = videoDate
    self.videoUrl = videoUrl
}
```

This is all the information we need for the video part. Now, we need to create the necessary attributes to store the audio information. The audio file, which is different from the video file, is a temporary file and should be created only when it is requested.

The file name will always be the same; this is the reason it should be constant. The full path is not constant as it contains an intermediate directory that can vary. Once the full path is set, we are also going to set the equivalent URL attribute, taking advantage of the `didSet` property observer. Place the following code to complete the `AssetInfo` audio attribute part:

```
let audioFilename = "rehash.m4a"
var audioPath:String? {
    didSet {
        if let audioPath = self.audioPath {
```

```
            self.audioUrl = NSURL(fileURLWithPath: audioPath)
        }else {
            self.audioUrl = nil
        }
    }
}

var audioUrl:NSURL?
```

To finish this class, we need to create a method that generates a temporary audio file with its full path. Technically speaking, it will create only a directory inside the temporary app directory, however, the file path will include the filename.

 Avoid creating temporary files or directories inside documents or library folders. These folders are backed up and sometimes copied to the Apple cloud, consuming space and broadband data.

Create a method called `prepareAudio`, which returns an optional NSURL that represents the full path for the audio file. In case of an error, this method shouldn't be responsible for letting the user know about it, therefore we have to let this method propagate the error to the function that called it. This is the reason this method has the `throws` keyword in its definition. Place the following method header to open the `prepareAudio` method:

```
func prepareAudio() throws -> NSURL? {
```

As this method needs to work with files and directories, we have to retrieve the file manager instance with the following code:

```
let fileManager = NSFileManager.defaultManager()
```

Now, we are going to create a unique name for the intermediate directory. To do it, we are going to call the `globallyUniqueString` attribute of the `processInfo` object. This attribute returns a string that is a combination of the hostname, the process id, and the timestamp, making it unique. Place the following code to create the intermediate directory:

```
let globallyUniqueString =
NSProcessInfo.processInfo().globallyUniqueString
let tempPath = (NSTemporaryDirectory() as
NSString).stringByAppendingPathComponent(globallyUniqueString)
try fileManager.createDirectoryAtPath(tempPath,
withIntermediateDirectories: false, attributes: nil)
```

The `try` statement is new in Swift 2 and it is mandatory when you call a method that throws exceptions. In this case, the exception will be propagated, as there is no do-catch statement and the method was declared with the `throws` attribute.

Eventually, you will use the `try` statement, followed by an exclamation mark (`try!`). It means that, in case of an error, it won't be propagated. There is another possibility, that is, the `try` statement, followed by a question mark (`try?`). It means that the exception won't be propagated and the returned value will be `nil`.

After creating the intermediate directory, we can set the full audio path and print a log with the full path. It can be helpful, while developing, to see whether everything is going fine. Place the following code to complete this method:

```
    self.audioPath = (tempPath as
NSString).stringByAppendingPathComponent(self.audioFilename)
        print("The full audio path is \(audioPath))")
        return self.audioUrl
    }
```

When should we clean this file? We can do it while destroying this object, as there will be no more use of this file. Thus, we must delete the file in the `deinit` method as follows. As there are no more methods of this class, we can close it:

```
    deinit {
        let fileManager = NSFileManager.defaultManager()
        do {
            if let audioPath = self.audioPath {
                try fileManager.removeItemAtPath(audioPath)
            }
        } catch {
            print("Couldn't delete \(self.audioPath!) on file
            \(__FILE__) at line \(__LINE__)")
        }
    }
} // end class AssetInfo
```

Listing videos

Let's start with the first scene, where the user will see, in the table view, a list of his/her videos. In this scene, we just need to add a label and a table view. Set the label title to **Choose your video** and place it at the top center of the screen. Under it, place the table view, occupying the rest of the screen. The final layout should be similar to the following screenshot:

Once you have the scene layout, go to its view controller file, import the `Photos` framework, and complete the class header by adding the `UITableViewDataSource` and `UITableViewDelegate` protocols. This is shown in the following highlighted code:

```
import Photos

class InitialViewController: UIViewController,
UITableViewDataSource, UITableViewDelegate {
```

 Photos is a framework that replaces Assets Library and it is available for iOS 8.0. Therefore, ensure that your deployment target is for iOS 8 or above while using this framework.

This class needs two attributes: one is the table view instance and the other is an array of `AssetInfo`, which contains each video's information. Add this code to the `InitialViewController` class:

```
@IBOutlet weak var assetsTableView: UITableView!
var assets = [AssetInfo]()
```

Once we have the attributes, we can initialize this class with the `viewDidLoad` method. Here, we have to check whether the user has already authorized the app to access the photo library. If we already have the authorization, we can initialize the assets by invoking a function that will be implemented afterwards, otherwise we will have to request authorization. Place the following implementation of `viewDidLoad` in your `InitialViewController` class:

```
override func viewDidLoad() {
    super.viewDidLoad()

    if PHPhotoLibrary.authorizationStatus() == .Authorized {
        self.initAssets()
    }
    else {
        PHPhotoLibrary.requestAuthorization({ (status:
        PHAuthorizationStatus) -> Void in
            switch status {
            case .Authorized:
                self.initAssets()
            default:
                print("Not authorized")
            }
        })
    }
}
```

Now we can implement the `initAssets` method. Here, we have to query for the videos in our photo library. To do it, we are going to use a method called `fetchAssetsWithMediaType` that belongs to `PHAsset`. Place the following code to open the `initAssets` method and to query videos from the photo library:

```
func initAssets(){
    self.assets = [AssetInfo]()
    let videos = PHAsset.fetchAssetsWithMediaType(.Video,
    options: nil)
```

The `videos` variable is of the `PHFetchResult` type, which has some similarities to an array, as it has the `count` property and you can use the subscript to access the elements. Once we have these concepts in mind, we can write the loop as follows:

```
for i in 0..<videos.count {
```

Each result should be an object of the `PHAsset` type, which still doesn't give us all the information we need; we still need the help of an object of the `PHImageManager` type. This object can search for the video equivalent, `AVAsset` object that will give us the video creation date and its URL. Type the following code to request the `AVAsset` objects and to initialize the `AssetInfo` object:

```
if let video = videos[i] as? PHAsset{
    let imageManager = PHImageManager.defaultManager()
    imageManager.requestAVAssetForVideo(video ,
    options: nil, resultHandler: { (asset: AVAsset?,
    _: AVAudioMix?, _:[NSObject : AnyObject]?) -> Void
    in
        if let urlAsset = asset as? AVURLAsset where
        urlAsset.playable {
            let date:String
            if let dateValue =
            urlAsset.creationDate?.dateValue{
                let formatter = NSDateFormatter()
                formatter.dateFormat = "dd-MM-yyyy"
                date =
                formatter.stringFromDate(dateValue)
            }else {
                date = "Unknown date"
            }
            let assetInfo = AssetInfo(videoDate: date,
            videoUrl: urlAsset.URL)
```

As you can see, `AVURLAsset` has inherited a property from `AVAsset` called `playable`. This property means that the asset can be used to initialize an instance of `AVPlayerItem`.

We still need one more object to complete the video part of our AssetInfo objects: the thumbnail. Again, we will need to use the image manager to request this object. The operation is similar to the previous one; however, this time we will use the requestImageForAsset method. Once it is done, we can add the assetInfo object to the array and reload the table view data in the main thread. Place this code to request the video thumbnail image and close the initAssets method:

```
imageManager.requestImageForAsset(video,
targetSize: CGSizeMake(64, 64),
contentMode:
PHImageContentMode.AspectFill, options:
nil, resultHandler: { (image:UIImage?,
_:[NSObject : AnyObject]?) -> Void in
    assetInfo.videoThumbnail = image
    self.assets.append(assetInfo)
    dispatch_async(dispatch_get_main_queue(),
{ () -> Void in

        self.assetsTableView.reloadData()
    })
})
        }
      })
    }
  }
} // end initAssets
```

The assets are loaded but the table view still doesn't display anything, as we haven't yet implemented the data source methods. The number of cells displayed should be the same as the assets array size. Therefore, you will have to paste the following code to implement numberOfRowsInSection:

```
func tableView(tableView: UITableView, numberOfRowsInSection
section: Int) -> Int{
    return assets.count
}
```

The next method is cellForRowAtIndexPath, where we can take the corresponding assetInfo object and return a cell that represents it. Place the following implementation for displaying the asset info cells:

```
func tableView(tableView: UITableView, cellForRowAtIndexPath
indexPath: NSIndexPath) -> UITableViewCell{
    var cell =
tableView.dequeueReusableCellWithIdentifier("assetcell")
        if cell == nil {
```

```
            cell = UITableViewCell(style: .Subtitle,
            reuseIdentifier: "assetcell")
        }

        let assetInfo = assets[indexPath.row]
        cell?.textLabel?.text = assetInfo.videoDate
        cell?.detailTextLabel?.text =
        assetInfo.videoUrl.absoluteString
        cell?.imageView?.image = assetInfo.videoThumbnail
        return cell!
    }
} // end InitialViewController
```

To finish this part of the app, you have to return to the storyboard, connect the table view data source and delegate to the view controller, and also connect the table view reference to the assetsTableView attribute.

Now you can test your app. It will ask for permission to use the photo library and display the list of videos on your phone. This test can be done on the simulator, however, you would have to add some videos to get a better result. If you are using any version control systems, it is a good time to commit your changes.

Recording

The first scene was created to let the user choose the video that he/she wanted to edit. Now, we have to create another scene where the user will watch the movie while recording his/her narrative over it.

Add a new file called RecorderViewController.swift to your project and import UIKit, AVFoundation, and Photos, as shown in the following code:

```
import UIKit
import AVFoundation
import Photos
```

Create a class called RecorderViewController, which inherits from UIViewController and implements the AVAudioRecorderDelegate protocol with the following code:

```
class RecorderViewController: UIViewController,
AVAudioRecorderDelegate {
```

This scene will have only a view, where the user will watch the movie, and a button to record the audio. Based on this information, we are going to add `UIView` and `UIButton` as attributes. Place the following code to add the needed UI attributes:

```
@IBOutlet weak var videoView: UIView!
@IBOutlet weak var recordButton: UIButton!
```

This class still needs more attributes, one of them is the `assetInfo` object that will be submitted from the previous class. Another one is an object of the `AVAudioRecorder` type that will use the device microphone to record the user's voice, an object of the `AVPlayer` type that will display the chosen video, and an `AVPlayerItem` object to control the player's status. Once we have understood these, we can add the following attributes:

```
var assetInfo:AssetInfo!
var recorder:AVAudioRecorder!
var player: AVPlayer!
var playerItem:AVPlayerItem!
```

Now we can implement the `viewDidLoad` method. In this case, we are just going to initialize the recorder object, as the asset info was transmitted from the previous class, and the player will be initialized when we start recording. Place the following code to implement `viewDidLoad`:

```
override func viewDidLoad() {
    super.viewDidLoad()
    self.initRecorder()
}
```

As you can see, you have to create a method called `initRecord` that will initialize the recorder attribute. The first step is to change the current audio category to `AVAudioSessionCategoryPlayAndRecord`, otherwise you are not going to be able to record. Changing the audio category will make the app request for permission to use the microphone. Place this code to start the `initRecord` method and change the audio session category:

```
private func initRecorder() {
    if let audioUrl = try! self.assetInfo.prepareAudio() {
        let session = AVAudioSession.sharedInstance()
        do {
            try session.setCategory(AVAudioSessionCategoryPlayAndRecord)
            try session.setActive(true)
```

Pay attention that we have to activate the session to use it. This step is mandatory as it will apply the configuration and make the session ready to use it.

The next step before instantiating the recorder is to create the recorder's settings. A recorder setting is just a dictionary and you can use some existing constants for the desired keys. Here, we are going to use a good quality audio setting; however, you can change it if you think that it is too much to just record someone's voice. Add this code to create the recorder's settings:

```
var recordSetting = [String:AnyObject]()
recordSetting[AVFormatIDKey] =
NSNumber(unsignedInt: kAudioFormatMPEG4AAC)
recordSetting[AVSampleRateKey] = 44100.0
recordSetting[AVNumberOfChannelsKey] = 2
```

The needed keys can vary according to the recording's format. Check Apple's documentation at https://developer.apple.com/library/ios/documentation/MusicAudio/Reference/CAFSpec/CAF_spec/CAF_spec.html if you would like to record using a different format.

Finally, we can instantiate the recorder, set it up, and enable the record button. Pay attention that the current object (self) is its delegate. We are doing it to detect when the recording is done. Place the following code to set up the recorder:

```
recorder = try AVAudioRecorder(URL: audioUrl,
settings: recordSetting)
recorder.delegate = self
recorder.meteringEnabled = true
recorder.prepareToRecord()
self.recordButton.enabled = true
```

The method is almost done; we just need to close the do statement with the corresponding catch statement and close some brackets till we close the method:

```
}catch {
    print("Fail to initialize the recorder. File
    \(__FILE__), Line: \(__LINE__)")
}
}
} // end initRecord
```

When the user presses the record button, we shall instantiate the player. To do it, we need an instance of an object of the AVPlayerItem type. This object observes the player's status, so we know when the player is ready to start playing the movie. Open the button touch up inside action with the following code:

```
@IBAction func startRecording(sender: UIButton) {
    // avoid letting the user press twice the same button.
```

```
sender.enabled = false
let asset = AVAsset(URL: self.assetInfo.videoUrl)
playerItem = AVPlayerItem(asset: asset)
```

The `AVPlayerItem` class follows the KVO pattern. It means that we have to add an observer to it through the `addObserver` method. Here, we just need to check when the status changes to ready, to play it. This status will eventually be reported in the method `observeValueForKeyPath`. Place the following code line to add the current object as an observer:

```
playerItem.addObserver(self, forKeyPath: "status",
options: .New, context: nil)
```

At this point, the app knows what to do when the video is loaded and ready to play, but it can't detect when the movie is over. To do it, we will have to detect it in a different way. In this case, we need to use the notification center and detect when the notification named `AVPlayerItemDidPlayToEndTimeNotification` is triggered. The `itemDidFinishPlaying` method (created by us) will then be called. Add this code to add the observer to the notification center:

```
NSNotificationCenter.defaultCenter().addObserver(self,
selector: Selector("itemDidFinishPlaying:"), name:
AVPlayerItemDidPlayToEndTimeNotification, object:
playerItem)
```

Once we have finished with the player item setup, we can instantiate the player. We specify that the video must pause when it reaches the end by using the following code:

```
player = AVPlayer(playerItem: playerItem)
player.actionAtItemEnd = AVPlayerActionAtItemEnd.Pause
```

The player is ready, but where is it going to display the movie? It must display it on the view called `videoView`, and it can be done thanks to a class called `AVPlayerLayer`. As the name says, this object must be added to the view as a sublayer, not as a subview. So, we will add the following code to create the video layer and close the `startRecording` method:

```
let playerLayer = AVPlayerLayer(player: player)
playerLayer.frame = self.videoView.bounds
self.videoView.layer.addSublayer(playerLayer)
}
```

What should the app do when the video is ready to be played? The answer is very easy; start playing the video and recording the audio, so the observeValueForKeyPath implementation is as simple as the following:

```
override func observeValueForKeyPath(keyPath: String?,
ofObject object: AnyObject?, change: [String : AnyObject]?,
context: UnsafeMutablePointer<Void>) {
    if let playerItem = object as? AVPlayerItem where
    playerItem.status == .ReadyToPlay {
        player.play()
        recorder.record()
    }else {
        super.observeValueForKeyPath(keyPath, ofObject:
        object, change: change, context: context)
    }
}
```

What happens when the movie is over? In this case, we just need to stop recording, which by consequence, will call the audio recorder delegate to notify it. So, the itemDidFinishPlaying method is implemented with this simple code:

```
func itemDidFinishPlaying(notification: NSNotification){
    recorder.stop()
}
```

When the recorder stops, the audioRecorderDidFinishRecording method, which belongs to the AVAudioRecorderDelegate protocol, will be called. The only thing we need to do is to check whether the recording is finished with no errors. If so, we have to call a method in charge of merging both the assets: the recorded audio and the displayed video. Put the following code to call the merge method:

```
func audioRecorderDidFinishRecording(recorder:
AVAudioRecorder, successfully flag: Bool) {
    if flag {
        self.merge()
    }else {
        print("Record failed")
    }
}
```

The `merge` method needs to use an object of the `AVMutableComposition` type, because this class is able to create a new asset by merging others. So, let's start this method by creating the composition object:

```
func merge() {
    do {
        let composition = AVMutableComposition()
```

The first part of our composition is the audio track. Here, we have to load the audio asset, retrieve its length, and create a new track based on both the variables. The `insertTimeRange` method will do this job for us with the following code:

```
// Audio part
let audioAsset = AVURLAsset(URL:
self.assetInfo.audioUrl!)
let audioTimeRange = CMTimeRangeMake(kCMTimeZero,
audioAsset.duration)
let compositionAudioTrack =
composition.addMutableTrackWithMediaType(AVMediaTypeAudio,
preferredTrackID: kCMPersistentTrackID_Invalid)
try
compositionAudioTrack.insertTimeRange(audioTimeRange, ofTrack:
audioAsset.tracksWithMediaType(AVMediaTypeAudio).first!, atTime:
kCMTimeZero)
```

The video track has a similar code, switching the audio constants with the video equivalent ones. But there is something very important to add here: the preferred transform. The `preferredTransform` property will keep the video with its orientation, otherwise you might get portrait videos converted into landscape. Add the video part with the following code:

```
//Video part
let videoAsset = AVURLAsset(URL: assetInfo.videoUrl)
let videoTimeRange = CMTimeRangeMake(kCMTimeZero,
videoAsset.duration)
let compositionVideoTrack =
composition.addMutableTrackWithMediaType(AVMediaTypeVideo,
preferredTrackID: kCMPersistentTrackID_Invalid)
let videoTrack =
videoAsset.tracksWithMediaType(AVMediaTypeVideo).first!
compositionVideoTrack.preferredTransform =
videoTrack.preferredTransform
try
compositionVideoTrack.insertTimeRange(videoTimeRange,
ofTrack: videoTrack, atTime: kCMTimeZero)
```

Now that we have the audio track and the video track, we need to create the output file. The `AssetInfo` class has a code to create a temporary audio file. Now, we have to create a similar code for the video output file. Firstly, we are going to get a unique ID for an intermediate directory. Then, we will create such a directory and create a URL for this directory with a file called `rehash-output.mov`. Place this code to prepare for the video output file:

```
// Video Output
let fileManager = NSFileManager.defaultManager()
let globallyUniqueString =
NSProcessInfo.processInfo().globallyUniqueString
let tempPath = (NSTemporaryDirectory() as
NSString).stringByAppendingPathComponent(globallyUniqueString)
try fileManager.createDirectoryAtPath(tempPath,
withIntermediateDirectories: false, attributes: nil)
let outputPath = (tempPath as
NSString).stringByAppendingPathComponent("rehash-output.mov")
let outputFileUrl = NSURL(fileURLWithPath: outputPath
```

Everything is ready to be merged. To do this task, we are going to create an object of the `AVAssetExportSession` type. This object will need the composition object as input and some information on the output. Knowing that the file extension is `.mov`, we still need to report to the export session that the output type is an Apple Quick Time movie.

The asset export session starts working when the `exportAsynchronouslyWithCompletionHandler` method is called. As its name says, it works asynchronously. Once the exportation is done, the handler passed as an argument will be called. Add the following code to set up the export session and start the composition:

```
// Fusion
let assetExport = AVAssetExportSession(asset:
composition, presetName:
AVAssetExportPresetHighestQuality)
assetExport?.outputFileType =
"com.apple.quicktime-movie"
assetExport?.outputURL = outputFileUrl
assetExport?.exportAsynchronouslyWithCompletionHandler({
() ->
Void in
```

Who is going to send the output video to the photos library? The answer is the `Photos` framework, again. The `PHPhotoLibrary` class can gives us an instance of the photo library and we can request changes by calling the `performChanges` method. This method receives two closures as an argument; the first one contains the desired changes and the second one is called when the changes are done.

For the changes closure, we just need to call the `creationRequestForAssetFromVideoAtFileURL` method that belongs to the `PHAssetChangeRequest` class. For the completion handler, we need to delete the file, because it is already uploaded to the photo library, and print a log message for now. So, here is the code that copies the final video in the photo library:

```
PHPhotoLibrary.sharedPhotoLibrary().performChanges({
() -> Void in
            PHAssetChangeRequest.creationRequestForAssetFromVi
deoAtFileURL(outputFileUrl)
            }, completionHandler: { (success:Bool,
            error:NSError?) -> Void in
                if success {
                    try!
                    fileManager.removeItemAtPath(outputPath)
                    print("Successful saved to photo
                    library")
                }else {
                    print("Couldn't save to photo
                    library")
                }
            })
```

The code is ready. Now, we just need to close the brackets till we close the method and the class:

```
            })
        } catch {
            print("Failed merging the audio and video")
        }
    } // end merge
} // end RecorderViewController
```

Finally, we can go to the storyboard and modify the visual part. Drag a new view controller to the storyboard. Go to its identity inspector and set its class to **RecorderViewController** and its **Storyboard ID** to **recorderviewcontroller**, as demonstrated in the following screenshot:

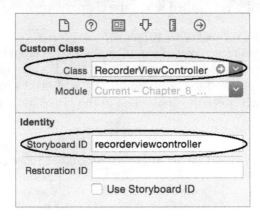

Place UIButton and UIView on the new scene. Set the button title to **Start recording**, place it at the bottom of the screen, and uncheck the enabled option on the attribute inspector. UIView can be placed at the center of the screen, occupying a size that you think that should be enough to display the video. But remember that a video can be landscape or portrait-oriented. The final layout should be similar to the following screenshot:

Connect the view to the `videoView` attribute as well as the button to the `recordButton` attribute and the `startRecording` action.

Can we test it now? No. If you do so, you are not going to see anything, as there is no action when you select a video on the first screen. Return to the `InitialViewController.swift` file and add the following method to call the next screen:

```
func tableView(tableView: UITableView, didSelectRowAtIndexPath
indexPath: NSIndexPath){
    if let recorderViewController =
self.storyboard?.instantiateViewControllerWithIdentifier("recorderview
controller") as? RecorderViewController {
        recorderViewController.assetInfo =
        assets[indexPath.row]
        self.presentViewController(recorderViewController,
        animated: true, completion: nil)
    }
}
```

Now you can test your app; remember that microphone input is a limitation of the iOS simulator, so it is better to test your app on a real device. Once you have recorded, you just have to wait till your log displays a message that the exportation is done. Then, you can go to the Photos app, check whether your video is there with today's date, and play it to hear your voice.

Improving the usability

So far, the app works and does what it is supposed to do, but we can still improve it. We should give the user the opportunity to return to the first screen and repeat the procedure with another video. Return to `InitialViewController` and add the following method that will reload the videos while returning to this view controller:

```
@IBAction func unwindToMainView(segue:UIStoryboardSegue) {
    self.initAssets()
}
```

Now, go to the storyboard and control-drag from the `RecorderViewController` icon to its exit icon, as shown in the following screenshot:

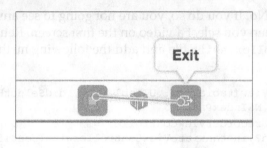

After releasing the mouse button, select the **unwindToMainView:** option. A new component with the **Unwind segue to Scene Exit Placeholder** phrase will appear on the document's outline. Click on it and go to its attribute inspector. In the **Identifier** field, set it to `exitrecorder`, as you can see in the following screenshot:

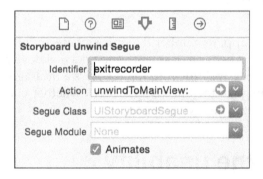

Now we can unwind to the main screen. To do it, we just need to return to the `merge` method and call the `performSegueWithIdentifier` method. Scroll down to where the `performChanges` method is performed and add the highlighted code at the end of its completion handler:

```
                PHPhotoLibrary.sharedPhotoLibrary().performChanges({
    () -> Void in
                PHAssetChangeRequest.creationRequestForAssetFromVi
    deoAtFileURL(outputFileUrl)
                }, completionHandler: { (success:Bool,
                error:NSError?) -> Void in
            if success {
                try!
                fileManager.removeItemAtPath(outputPath)
                print("Successful saved to photo
                library")
            }else {
```

```
                              print("Couldn't save to photo
                              library")
                      }
                      // Add the following code
                      dispatch_async(dispatch_get_main_queue(), {
                      () -> Void in
                              self.performSegueWithIdentifier("exitrecor
der", sender: self)
                      })
              })
```

If you test now, the app will crash when the movie is over, as it will detect that the player item still has an observer when destroyed. We can remove the observer before calling performSegueWithIdentifier, but a better place is on the deinit method, as it will always remove the observers when the current object is released. Add the following deinit implementation at the end of the RecorderViewController class:

```
deinit {
        self.playerItem.removeObserver(self, forKeyPath: "status")
        NSNotificationCenter.defaultCenter().removeObserver(self.
playerItem)
    }
```

Now you can test the app. Choose a video, record your voice over it, and when it finishes, check whether the app returns to the main screen and your new video is there.

Summary

In this chapter, you learned how to edit a video using AVFoundation, which is a low-level framework and allows us to merge audios and videos. We could play a video using AVPlayer and AVPlayerItem and record the sound using AVAudioSession. We used different classes to create the final product (the merged video) such as AVURLAsset and AVMutableComposition.

You also learned how to retrieve a list of videos from the photo library using a new framework called Photos. Once the final video was ready, we used the Photos framework to submit the video to the photo library.

This is the last chapter. I hope the you enjoyed the book.

Index

Thank you for buying
Swift 2 Blueprints

About Packt Publishing

Packt, pronounced 'packed', published its first book, *Mastering phpMyAdmin for Effective MySQL Management*, in April 2004, and subsequently continued to specialize in publishing highly focused books on specific technologies and solutions.

Our books and publications share the experiences of your fellow IT professionals in adapting and customizing today's systems, applications, and frameworks. Our solution-based books give you the knowledge and power to customize the software and technologies you're using to get the job done. Packt books are more specific and less general than the IT books you have seen in the past. Our unique business model allows us to bring you more focused information, giving you more of what you need to know, and less of what you don't.

Packt is a modern yet unique publishing company that focuses on producing quality, cutting-edge books for communities of developers, administrators, and newbies alike. For more information, please visit our website at www.packtpub.com.

About Packt Open Source

In 2010, Packt launched two new brands, Packt Open Source and Packt Enterprise, in order to continue its focus on specialization. This book is part of the Packt Open Source brand, home to books published on software built around open source licenses, and offering information to anybody from advanced developers to budding web designers. The Open Source brand also runs Packt's Open Source Royalty Scheme, by which Packt gives a royalty to each open source project about whose software a book is sold.

Writing for Packt

We welcome all inquiries from people who are interested in authoring. Book proposals should be sent to author@packtpub.com. If your book idea is still at an early stage and you would like to discuss it first before writing a formal book proposal, then please contact us; one of our commissioning editors will get in touch with you.

We're not just looking for published authors; if you have strong technical skills but no writing experience, our experienced editors can help you develop a writing career, or simply get some additional reward for your expertise.

Learning Swift

ISBN: 978-1-78439-250-5   Paperback: 266 pages

Build a solid foundation in Swift to develop smart and robust iOS and OS X applications

1. Practically write expressive, understandable, and maintainable Swift code.

2. Discover and optimize the features of Swift to write cleaner and better code.

3. This is a step-by-step guide full of practical examples to create efficient IOS applications.

Mastering Swift

ISBN: 978-1-78439-215-4   Paperback: 358 pages

Master Apple's new Swift programming language by following the best practices to write efficient and powerful code

1. Start with basic language features and progressively move to more advanced features.

2. Learn to use Xcode's new Playground feature as you work through the immense number of examples in the book.

3. Learn what makes development with Swift so exiting and also get pointers on pitfalls to avoid.

Please check **www.PacktPub.com** for information on our titles

open source
community experience distilled

Swift by Example

ISBN: 978-1-78528-470-0   Paperback: 284 pages

Create funky, impressive applications using Swift

1. Learn Swift language features quickly, with playgrounds and in-depth examples.

2. Implement real iOS apps using Swift and Cocoapods.

3. Create professional video games with SpriteKit, SceneKit, and Swift.

Learning iOS 8 Game Development Using Swift

ISBN: 978-1-78439-355-7   Paperback: 366 pages

Create robust and spectacular 2D and 3D games from scratch using Swift – Apple's latest and easy-to-learn programming language

1. Create engaging games from the ground up using SpriteKit and SceneKit.

2. Boost your game's visual performance using Metal - Apple's new graphics library.

3. A step-by-step approach to exploring the world of game development using Swift.

Please check **www.PacktPub.com** for information on our titles

www.ingramcontent.com/pod-product-compliance
Lightning Source LLC
Chambersburg PA
CBHW060529060326

40690CB00017B/3431

* 9 7 8 1 7 8 3 9 8 0 7 6 5 *